MW00454307

Case Studies and Activities in Adult Education and Human Resource Development

A volume in
Adult Education Special Topics:
Theory, Research, and Practice in Lifelong Learning

Series Editor
Kathleen P. King, *University of South Florida*

Adult Education Special Topics: Theory, Research, and Practice in Lifelong Learning

Kathleen P. King, Series Editor

Innovations in Career and Technical Education:
Strategic Approaches Toward Workforce Competencies Around the Globe (2007)
edited by Victor C. X. Wang and Kathleen P. King

Building Workforce Competencies in Career and Technical Education (2008)
edited by Victor C. X. Wang and Kathleen P. King

Fundamentals of Human Performance and Training (2008)
edited by Victor C. X. Wang and Kathleen P. King

Human Performance Models Revealed in the Global Context (2008)
edited by Victor C. X. Wang and Kathleen P. King

Empowering Women Through Literacy: Views From Experience (2009)
edited by Mev Miller and Kathleen P. King

The Handbook of the Evolving Research of Transformative Learning:
Based on the Learning Activities Survey (10th Anniversary Edition) (2009)
edited by Kathleen P. King

The Power of Learning From Inquiry: Teacher Research
as a Professional Development Tool in Multilingual Schools (2010)
by Aida A. Nevárez-La Torre

Case Studies and Activities in Adult Education and Human Resource Development

by

Steven W. Schmidt
East Carolina University

Information Age Publishing, Inc.
Charlotte, North Carolina • www.infoagepub.com

Library of Congress Cataloging-in-Publication Data

Schmidt, Steven W.
    Case studies and activities in adult education and human resource
development / by Steven W. Schmidt.
        p. cm. — (Adult education special topics: theory, research, and
practice in lifelong learning)
    Includes bibliographical references.
    ISBN 978-1-61735-073-3 (paperback) — ISBN 978-1-61735-074-0 (hardcover) —
ISBN 978-1-61735-075-7 (e-book)
    1. Adult education—United States—Case studies. 2. Manpower
policy—United States—Case studies. 3. Case method. I. Title.
    LC5251.S33 2010
    374'.973—dc22

                                                                    2010018433

Printed in the United States of America

CONTENTS

FOREWORD

Last semester (Fall 2009) I bit the pedagogical bullet and decided to use case studies extensively in my management of education courses. I talk about the experience as risk taking because for the learners and me, it was.

Using case studies as a primary instructional strategy is not customary in education, adult education, and human resources development courses, although case studies have been popular in other disciplines for many years. But the fact they have not been used a great deal in our fields means that by introducing case studies we have to help students become comfortable with and understand what they are and how to use them. The beginning of the semester was rough because the students were unsettled with the change of routine. However by midsemester they were in the groove, and at the end of term I had a classroom "converted" to case study instructional methods.

When Dr. Steven Schmidt and I started discussing his interest in developing this book, I immediately saw the need and value for a case study guide and resource. Some areas of study have case study books readily available, for instance higher education, business, and law, but in the fields of adult education and human resource development, we could not find any. The result is that teachers and professors have to create their own from scratch for every class, subject, and objective they teach. There has to be a better way.

I believe Dr. Schmidt has created an immensely valuable resource for trainers, professors, and instructors with this volume. Not only does he

Case Studies and Activities in Adult Education and Human Resources Development
pp. ix–xi
Copyright © 2010 by Information Age Publishing
ix

walk us through how to think about, plan, introduce, and facilitate case studies with adult students in our discipline areas, but he also has gathered some of the very best examples from scores of expert colleagues in the field of study.

The breadth of specific topic areas addressed in this volume is a staggering and exciting discovery.

- In adult education, the cases include adult basic education and literacy, teaching, administration, instructional design, and community education.
- In human resource development, topics for cases encompass program development, organizational development, training, workplace diversity, cross-cultural communication, management development, and internal resources.
- Both areas are addressed by cases ranging across the subjects of needs assessment, program planning and evaluation, career development, work/life issues, ethics, continuing professional development, the adult learner, and general classroom activities.

Why are case studies such an effective instructional strategy? In part because they incorporate both many higher order thinking skills, and leverage application to real-life contexts. The blend of situated learning with problem solving, critical thinking, analysis, and decision making connect theoretical content with lived experience and brings out the complexities inherent in that subject. So very consistent with advanced study of our content areas as well, case studies do not isolate facts, theories, and concepts to separate silos or domains. Instead, students and teachers alike must bring all their understanding of the content area to bear on the situation, see how the different aspects that they know complement, confirm, and even contradict! Add to the fact that often we use case studies in small and large group settings and powerful opportunities to develop and hone collaborative learning, communication, negotiation, and persuasive skills are added to the mix.

If you are looking for a way to spark in-depth, on-topic discussions, to engage your students in thinking more deeply and critically about the subject area, and to advance in their transfer of learning, case studies are a necessary tool in your instructional strategy repertoire. And if you are looking for well-developed, detailed cases which will drive and cultivate critical thinking, research, and problem-solving and decision-making skills to the next level—this book is a treasure trove of selections for many different subject areas in our fields.

Thank you, Steven and the many contributing expert authors who have created this invaluable resource. You have filled a void which will improve our teaching and learning and increase the adoption of case studies as valuable instructional strategies.

Kathleen P. King
Professor of Education
University of South Florida
Tampa, FL
June 2010

CHAPTER 1

INTRODUCTION TO CASE STUDIES

Life is a case study. We may not be aware of it on a daily basis, but we are all characters in the case studies of our lives and in the lives of others with whom we interact. How often throughout the day do we analyze our actions, wish we would have done something different, reconsider and reframe situations to understand different viewpoints, or simply reflect on things that have happened? In that sense, our lives are an ongoing case study, and we make many decisions based on how we interpret the outcomes of past "cases" or situations.

We may not consider the term case study when we think of those situations. In some cases, they are stories that we repeat to interested parties, or that are passed along from someone else. In other cases, they are scenarios that we play back in our minds after having been exposed to a situation or event. The bottom line is that we spend a good deal of time examining peoples' lives, organizations or businesses, and general situations. In doing so, we are essentially looking at them in the context of a case study. We consider things like how individuals acted or reacted when faced with opportunities or challenges, how organizations performed in response to competition, and how groups of people came together to solve problems.

Think about how many times during the course of a day we reflect on the actions of a colleague, or customer or boss, or the direction taken by a

Case Studies and Activities in Adult Education and Human Resources Development
pp. 1–19
Copyright © 2010 by Information Age Publishing
1

group or organization. Those actions may be agreeable or disagreeable to us. They may be great or small in scope. They may affect one person or many thousands of people. Chances are, you evaluated what went wrong and what went well; or perhaps thought about what you might have done differently. Regardless of the circumstance, we are continually evaluating the "case studies" or scenarios to which we are exposed on a daily basis. Although mostly on informal bases, case studies are part of our everyday lives.

THE STORIES OF OUR LIVES

In many ways, case studies are stories. They may include narratives, descriptions of events and actions, and results or consequences that may have occurred. However, case studies can be more complex than stories—or they could be considered specific types of stories. They typically include some type of problem to be solved or lesson to be learned. They encourage the reader to ponder a situation or consider what he or she might do under similar circumstances. They can serve as examples of best, worst, or typical practice. We sometimes associate specific organizations or people with case study-approaches to certain topics. The retailer Nordstrom is a case study in the value of providing superior customer service. The women's liberation movement in the 1970s was a case study in the power of social movements. The website Facebook can be looked at as a case study in the development of online social interaction. *The Diary of Anne Frank* is a case study in the resilience and survival of people thrust into the most terrible of circumstances. Tina Turner's 50-plus year career in the music business is a case study in celebrity longevity. In these examples, we look at the strategies used, the paths taken, and the decisions made that resulted in these people, organizations, and movements transitioning from point A to point B.

Sometimes the term case study is used to describe a textbook or typical example. Organizations that want to be known for superior customer service should do the same things that Nordstrom does with regard to customer service. Barack Obama's 2008 presidential campaign was a case study in the power of grass-roots organization and individual involvement. Future political campaigns will no doubt be examining this approach when developing campaign strategies. Other times, it is used to describe an extreme example. The September 11, 2001, terrorist hijacking of airplanes that were then crashed into the World Trade Center buildings was a case study in the exploitation of gaps found in a variety of organizations and systems. Many actual case study examples in airport and airline security, communication, crisis management, and other topics used in classrooms today have come from that single event.

As you see from the above examples, case studies can feature both positive and negative outcomes. They can be examples of what to do, and of what not to do. They can teach us what to avoid and what to embrace. They can teach us what to consider and what to ignore. Using case studies, we can learn from both the positive steps and the mistakes of others without having to actually do anything other than analyze the case study.

WHAT IS A CASE STUDY?

Scholars have defined the concept of the case study in several ways. Erskine, Leenders, and Mauffette-Leenders (1981, cited in Herreid, 2006) defined a case study like this:

> A case is a description of an actual situation, commonly involving a decision, a challenge, an opportunity, a problem or an issue faced by a person or persons in an organization. The case requires the reader to step figuratively into the position of a particular decision maker (Herreid, 2006, p. 50).

Case studies require the reader to step into the situation itself. This thought is mirrored in Ellet's (2007) definition of a case study. "Case studies are verbal representations of reality that put the reader in the role of participant in the situation. (Their purpose is) to represent reality, to convey a situation with all its cross-currents and rough edges. They may be lengthy or short, and may provide many or few details" (p. 2). According to Ellet (2007), case studies share three common characteristics:

1. Focus on a significant issue.
2. Enough information for the reader or case participant to draw conclusions.
3. No stated conclusions of their own (Ellet, 2007, p. 2).

FACT OR FICTION?

Should case studies be based on actual events? It should be no surprise that there is some disagreement as to this issue among the academics who study case methods. Herreid (2006) notes that "A case study must be real. No lies. No fabrications. No fantasy. It must involve real events, real problems, and real people. Nothing is made up" (p. 50). However, others are not as strict in their definitions. "Case methods are often actual descriptions of problem situations in the field in which the case is being used; sometimes they are syntheses constructed to represent a particular principle or type of problem" (McKeachie & Svinicki, 2006, p. 223). It may be true that some case studies are based solely on actual events. Case studies involving businesses, for example, may include business names and actual statistics on profits, losses, and dollars spent on certain initiatives.

In other disciplines, it may not be possible to develop case studies that are entirely truthful. Medical case studies, for example, cannot use actual patient names and personal data. Case studies involving children, in primary education for example, typically use only first names, and often those names are changed to protect the actual students. Some writers believe case studies can be based on actual events, or hypothetical scenarios. They can also be a combination of real-world events that have been modified to highlight a specific problem or issue. In fact, sometimes the best case studies come from combinations of events that may not have occurred together, but make for thought-provoking situations.

The cases in this book typically fall into the latter category. Because they involve learning and learners, specific details have been changed to protect those learners. In some cases, we have modified situations to make cases more clear, and in other cases, we have combined actual scenarios to make the case more compelling and more challenging.

A CHUNK OF REALITY?

Regardless of how factual or made up the case study is, it must be accurate and real-sounding to the reader. It must be interesting enough to motivate consideration and thought. It must also have had the potential to have been an actual situation if readers are to take it seriously and become engaged in its study. The more participants believe a case study, the more likely they are to engage in the examination of the details of the case and to develop plausible solutions for the case. Lawrence (cited in Wasserman, 1994) describes a good case study as "the vehicle by which a chunk of reality is brought into the classroom to be worked over by the class and the instructor (p. 215). That "chunk of reality" can include details that are complex and often contradictory. It can feature characters with competing agendas and different perspectives on the issues to be examined. Just like in real life, facts, emotions, needs, and motivations all come into play in different ways. In short, good case studies are multidimensional and detailed scenarios that provide a foundation for discussion and problem solving.

Ten Second Tip

Whether fact, fiction, or some combination thereof, a case study must be believable to the reader.

Figure 1.1.

WHAT MAKES A GOOD CASE?

"Case methods are intended to develop student ability to solve problems using knowledge, concepts, and skills relevant to a course" (McKeachie & Svinicki, 2006, p. 223). Problem solving is important, so cases typically include the following:

- Multiple paths to take.
- Choices to be made along the way.
- Interplay among variables.
- A variety of possible solutions.

Each possible solution to a case comes with different positives and negatives to be weighed by the participant as well. To mimic a real-world environment, case studies can also include extra information that is not relevant to the case in any way. This extra information or "noise" is also characteristic of problem solving in the real world. "Many cases have elaborate padding in the text, and exhibits that serve as noise to distract the reader and make it harder to distinguish the useful information" (Ellet, 2007, p. 4). All case studies feature some degree of ambiguity as well. Not all important information is stated, and as a result, participants must make inferences or assumptions based on what is known. Like the real

Ten Second Tip

Good case studies never include correct or incorrect answers.

Figure 1.2.

world, information included in case studies is not presented in an orderly fashion. Rather, the reader must pull key pieces of information from throughout the case itself.

TYPES OF CASE STUDIES

Case studies are typically developed with different goals and objectives in mind. It stands to reason, then, that not all case studies are alike. Simmons (1974, cited in Armistead, 1984) has identified several different categories of case studies:

- **The exercise case study** provides an opportunity for the student to practice the application of specific procedures.
- **The situation case study** is the type most generally associated with the term case study. The student is asked to analyze the information in the case.
- **The complex case study** is an extension of the situation case study. The student is required to handle a large amount of data and information, some of which is irrelevant.
- **The decision case study** requires the student to go a step further than in the previous category and present plans for solving a problem.
- **The in-basket case study** is a particular type of decision case study. The student is presented with a collection of documents and background information and is expected to record the actions he or she would take relating to each document, some of which will be interrelated.
- **The critical incident case study** provides the student with a certain amount of information and withholds other information until it is requested by the student.
- **The action maze case study** presents a large case study in a series of small units. The student is required at each stage to predict what will happen next.
- **The role play case study** requires the student and perhaps the case leader to assume roles in the case (Armistead, 1984, p. 75).

WHY STUDY CASES?

Many of you have spent countless hours in the classroom, either as an instructor or student. You know that when developing curriculum or considering course activities, instructors have all kinds options from which to choose. We use lectures, experiential learning activities, group work, writing-based exercises, self-study, or a variety of other methods to help students learn. With all these options available, why choose case studies? There are several reasons for opting to use case studies as an instructional strategy. Case studies can be a catalyst for active participation in a classroom. They can get students involved and discussion flowing. Many researchers point to the positive relationship between student involvement in the classroom and learning. "The relationship between learning and involvement is so strong and positive that researchers sometimes use estimates of involvement as proxy measures for learning; that is, when they observe students involved, they assume these students are learning" (McNergney, Ducharme, & Ducharme, 1999, p. 5). This is an important point: The more students are actively involved in classroom activities, the more they are learning.

Case studies can promote that involvement. They "allow deliberation, reflection, discussion, and collaboration that are not always possible in a real setting" (Campoy, 2005, p. 7). Case studies are flexible in that they can be tailored by the instructor to match the instructional goals. They can bridge the gap between theory and practice in the sense that they provide students the opportunity to apply theory to practice. They benefit from the diversity of a classroom, in that all learners can bring their varying degrees of experience to the table and learn from each other. They allow students time to consider alternatives and make choices in the relatively safe environment of the classroom, as opposed to having to make those same types of decisions in the real world, where stakes may be higher and decisions must be made faster. One researcher examined the use of case studies among preservice teachers, and concluded that "Through vicarious engagement in case stories, preservice teachers make discoveries about themselves as future teachers and as learners. Using cases also enables preservice teachers to discover how colleagues' perspectives, values, and ideas may influence changes in their understanding of teaching and learning" (Lundeburg, Levin, & Harrington, 1999, p. xviii). While this researcher's study focused on one group of learners, we can probably generalize the results to all who study cases.

The continual study of cases over time can also be beneficial to students. As is the case with many educational activities, the ongoing examination and analysis of cases as part of an overall program of study is helpful in the learning process. "The repetitive opportunity to identify, analyze, and solve a number of cases in a variety of settings prepares learners to become truly professionals in their field of work" (Herreid, 2006, p. 50).

In summary, the benefits of using case studies are as follows:

- They promote active class participation;
- They can be tailored to match instructional goals;
- They can bridge the gap between theory and practice;
- Students bring their own experiences to the case and can learn from each other;
- They allow students to make choices and consider alternatives in a safe environment; and
- Over time, they help students develop analysis skills.

THE HISTORY OF CASE STUDIES

Learning from case studies, often in the form of stories, is not new. In fact, we have been doing it for thousands of years. The earliest societies used stories to share knowledge and to teach others. Knowledge was passed from generation to generation in the form of stories and scenarios that enabled future generations to make advances to many aspects of life. Knowledge of how to gather food, how and when to plant certain crops, and how to hunt was passed along from generation to generation. The lessons learned through those stories are similar to the conclusions or solutions of a case study. Those stories may not have been as complex as case studies we know today, but they were similar in the sense that knowledge was gained through the evaluation of a scenario and through the decisions made as a result of that knowledge.

The Innovator: Law

As people progressed and advanced through time, so too did the study of cases as a way to learn. The study of cases on a formal level began in 1870 at Harvard Law School (Merseth, 1991). The law school, headed by Christopher Columbus Langdell, was facing a series of difficulties associated with the teaching of the law discipline itself. At that time, the study of law was not seen as legitimate in higher education. "The legal literature was immense, disorganized, and thus confusing to students and faculty alike" (McNergney et al., 1999, p. 7) and the teaching of law was viewed as something that could be accomplished in an apprenticeship rather than through formal academic training. Langdell proposed the case-study approach to "generalize particular decisions into broader understanding of the principles of the law" (Merseth, 1991, p. 243). Case studies were incorporated into the Harvard Law School curriculum, and despite initial skepticism by faculty at other law schools, were a success. By 1915, the case study method was being used by most of the well-known law schools of the time (Merseth, 1991).

The Early Adopters: Medicine and Business

Shortly after its use began at Harvard, a variation of the case study methodology was implemented at Johns Hopkins Medical School. In 1893, the school introduced an approach to medical education that consisted of two years of traditional classroom and laboratory instruction, followed by two years of experience training in a clinic alongside experienced practitioners. "Students followed the progress of a number of patients until they were discharged or died. [These students] learned to examine, diagnose, and treat actual patients, and this hands-on approach to medical education provided the foundation for the case methodology still used in medical schools today (McNergney et al., 1999, p. 7).

During the time its law school was finding success with the case study method, the Harvard Business School was created and had started taking shape. Those involved in the creation of the business school recognized the success of the case study method at the law school, and sought to develop a similar format for their business school. In 1908 the Harvard Graduate School of Business Administration was established, and its curriculum featured the case study approach as its primary instructional method. While the Harvard Law School relied on actual court decisions as bases for its case studies, the Business School did not have comparable materials upon which to build cases. Furthermore, the Business School faculty lacked the expertise and understanding of the case study method necessary to successfully implement it in the classroom.

Implementation of the case study method in the Business School lagged until 1919, when a new dean took over as head of that school (Merseth, 1991). Wallace B. Donham was a graduate of Harvard Law, and as a result, he understood case-based instruction. He immediately began working on two initiatives that he believed would help the Business School effectively incorporate case-based learning. The first involved support for faculty transitioning to teaching using the case study method. Best-practice groups, formal and informal meetings, and other types of training sessions helped faculty become comfortable teaching via the case study method (Merseth, 1999). Interestingly enough, it seems that many of the methods chosen by Donham actually resulted in faculty learning by using their own experiences in the classroom as case studies.

Lack of business-related case studies was still a problem for the school. To address that issue, Donham founded the Bureau of Business Research; an organization set up specifically to collect actual information from businesses and to develop business-related case studies with that information. Research conducted by the Bureau was funneled directly to the business school, where faculty developed case studies around the Bureau's research (Lockley, 1950). Motivating faculty to actually write the case studies was possible because the school broadened the concept of faculty research to include the development and writing of case studies. Business school faculty were required to develop case studies and related materials as part of their positions, and worked with the Bureau on the development of case materials (Merseth, 1999). Through this combination of efforts, Donham was successful in implementing the case study approach in the Harvard School of Business. Gradually other schools of business adopted the method, and it is now a standard feature of many business school courses and programs.

The Late Majority: Education

Compared to medicine, law, and business, the discipline of education was slower to adopt and accept of the case study method. The use of the case studies in education started in the 1920s in teacher education programs in New Jersey and Massachusetts. Case studies have been used to teach both business and law-related topics in educational administration since the mid 1950s, and "Although activities related to this pedagogical approach in the field of education were never large or particularly well organized, they nevertheless existed in a steady state throughout the 1960s and 1970s (Lundeberg et al., 1999, p. 8).

Why the lag in the use of case studies in education when it was becoming so popular in other disciplines? Some researchers point to the lack of adequate case records or situations suitable for use in the classroom (accompanied by a lack of resources necessary to develop those case studies). Lack of consensus by education professionals as to how case studies should be used in the classroom was another factor. Some in academia believed that education had not developed issues broad enough for case studies to be useful. However, several movements arose starting in the 1980s that would challenge these notions that hindered the use of case studies in education.

The school reform movement in the 1980s, the advocacy of the case-based approach by a variety of educational associations, and the increased awareness of the importance of teachers all served to pique interest in the use of cased-based methods of instruction. "Since the mid-1990s, the tone

	Ten Second Tip
	Case studies help learners to prepare for complex and ambiguous situations similar to those they may encounter in the real world.

Figure 1.3.

and nature of the literature about the use of cases and case methods in teacher education has changed. Today's work in the field seems to reflect a much greater awareness about the need to understand, thorough empirical research, the appeal as well as the effect of this approach" (Lundeberg et al., 1999). Those in education came to realize that case studies help students frame educational issues in a context more closely related to what they would actually encounter in the real world. They realized that the use of case studies would help prepare students for difficult situations they would face in the classroom, and would help students see those situations from multiple perspectives. "The teaching case study helps students realize that the world is more complex than they expected it to be, and they become more prepared emotionally for a world where things do not always work out as students think they should" (Kleinfeld, 1990, p. 50 cited in McNergney et al., 1999, p. 9).

CASE STUDIES TODAY

Today, case studies are widely-used educational tools. From business to law to education to many other disciplines, learning from case studies goes on in a variety of different classrooms and on a variety of subjects. Case study learning today has grown far beyond its roots in law and medicine. Curriculum for careers in police science, and other technical and trade occupations includes the use of case studies as well. In his book on firefighting strategies, Avillo (2008) notes that "There is probably no other profession where case study is more valuable than in the fire service. In the case study method, details of past incidents are reviewed. Using this method, opportunities to learn arise from every emergency" (p. xxxi). Experts in many other occupations might substitute their occupations for that of "fire service" in the previous quotation and believe the statement to be correct. And in many cases, they would be right.

Case studies are used in educational settings beyond traditional higher education as well. Business and industry and nonprofit organizations are some of the groups that have found the use of case studies beneficial in employee training programs and corporate universities. The German corporation Siemens uses problems it encounters in the course of doing business in its "Siemens University"; the company's in-house corporate training program. Rather than hire consultants to address multilayered and complex issues the company is facing, those issues end up in Siemens University, "where Siemens analysts and engineers act like MBA students and use Siemens' business problems as case studies to be solved" (p. xx). Ewing (1999) notes that "Siemens may be one of the only companies in the world whose management education program not only pays for itself but also saves the company money" (p. xx). That savings amounted to about $11 million in 1999 (Ewing).

Learning from past situations, from scenarios, from mistakes that have been made and from good ideas that have been implemented successfully is what the case study method is all about. The philosopher George Santayana wrote that "Those who do not learn from history are doomed to repeat it." While Santayana may not have been referring specifically to the case study method in education, it does apply. Educators in many disciplines have found that case studies allow us to learn from history, whether that history is many years or a few minutes old.

THE THEORY BEHIND THE CASE

At this point, you may be thinking that case studies could be effective tools in the classroom. You might also be wondering why they can be effective. This is where the connection of theory to practice comes in, so be forewarned that this section contains a lot of theoretical terms and concepts.

Constructivist Theory.   The use of case studies as learning tools is based in the concept of several learning theories. Case-based learning is an example of a constructivist approach to education (McNergney et. al., 1999). Constructivists believe learning is a process of constructing meaning. It is how people make sense of their experiences (Merriam & Caffarella, 1999). In order to construct that meaning, those experiences have to be separated, considered and reflected upon. In that way, we construct knowledge.

Because the process of construction is unique to each individual, a constructivist would tell you that the concept of reality is also unique to each individual (and that there is no one absolute reality for everyone). What is more applicable to we who use case studies is the following information: Constructivists believe that problems are not solved by the retrieval of rote-learned "right" answers. Rather, to solve a problem intelligently, you

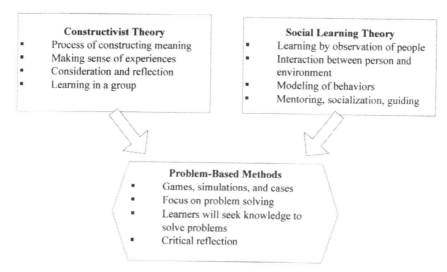

Constructivist Theory
- Process of constructing meaning
- Making sense of experiences
- Consideration and reflection
- Learning in a group

Social Learning Theory
- Learning by observation of people
- Interaction between person and environment
- Modeling of behaviors
- Mentoring, socialization, guiding

Problem-Based Methods
- Games, simulations, and cases
- Focus on problem solving
- Learners will seek knowledge to solve problems
- Critical reflection

Figure 1.4.

must first see it as your own problem. Does that sound in line with the case study approach? All these elements of constructivism are evident in the case study approach. The instructor guides the student through various scenarios and approaches, examining different possibilities and hypothesizing about potential outcomes. In summary, important elements of constructivist teaching that are common in the case study approach include group learning, and experience and reflection, and the process of making or constructing meaning (Von Glaserfelt, 1995), although the experience and reflection involved in studying cases may be more hypothetical than actual.

Social Learning Theory.   Elements of social learning theory are important as a theoretical basis in case study analysis. Social learning theorists focus on learning from the observation of other people in social settings. That learning happens with the interaction of the person, the environment and the person's behavior. If you were to talk to a social learning theorist, he or she would tell you that effective social learning involves modeling of behaviors and interaction with other people and the environment. The ability to understand generalizations, yet pay attention to detail in these interactions is also important. Social learning theorists stress concepts such as mentoring, socialization, and guiding as part of learning processes (Bandura & Walters, 1963). Can you see the connections between social learning theory and the use of the case study method?

In the case study method, social learning theory is applicable on two levels. Students may learn from the actions of the characters in the case study. Remember that in order to be effective, case studies must be seen as actually possible to have occurred in the real world (if they are not already based on actual facts). In effective cases, students are able to position themselves in the case, as actual characters in that case. In doing so, the student learns from the actions of other characters in the case itself, and from the actions of those other characters in the case. Based on the actions of those other characters, the students make decisions in response to situations that present themselves in the case.

On another level, social learning theory is applicable in the study of cases in the classroom environment. Classroom activities, whether they take place in traditional face-to-face or online classrooms, typically involve the discussion of case studies among students. It is that discussion among students, all of whom bring different points of view to the situation, that can make case study discussions rich classroom activities. Students learn from the thoughts expressed by their classmates, from the perspectives from which they view the case, and from the experiences of other students that lead to those students' statements and conclusions. In this interaction, they may be just as likely to learn what to do as what not to do. During this discussion, the facilitator acts as a mentor or guide. He or she may summarize points made by students, highlight trends noted, and reframe statements to allow students to view situations from different perspectives as well. All of these activities related to case study facilitation are in keeping with the principles of social learning theory as well.

The case study method is based on both constructivist and social learning theory. Switching gears from theory, the method itself is one of several that are categorized as problem-based educational methods.

Problem-Based Education

The case study approach is one of several educational methods that fall under the general category of problem-based approaches to learning. Games, activities, simulations, and case studies all fall in the category of problem-based education. "Problem-based education is based on the assumptions that human beings evolved as individuals who are motivated to solve problems, and that problem solvers will seek and learn whatever knowledge is needed for successful problem solving" (McKeachie & Svinicki, 2006, p. 222). Notice the connection between problem-based learning and constructivist theories described in the prior section.

	Ten Second Tip
	The use of case studies and other problem-based approaches to learning is rooted in several educational theories, including constructivism and social learning theory.

Figure 1.5.

A major goal of problem-based learning is to promote the development of clinical reasoning or problem-solving skills in students. Through continuous exposure to real-life problems and modeling provided by an instructor, mentor, or coach, students will acquire the craft of evaluating problems, deciding what's wrong, and making decisions about appropriate courses of action (Norman & Schmidt, 1992). Although Norman and Schmidt's (1992) comments regarding problem-based learning are in the context of medical education, they do have general applications.

In the preceding sections, you may have noticed that the concept of reflecting on situations and actions keeps reappearing. However, no new learning occurs if you reflect on things the same way, using the same thought processes, all the time. You must use a critical eye in that reflection if you are to learn from it. The process of using that critical eye, also known as critical reflection, is important in learning from case studies. One key element of critical reflection, especially important when reviewing the information presented in a case study, is the examination of our own views and assumptions when we read that information. The connection between learning and critical reflection can be viewed this way:

> Learning may be defined as the process of making a new or revised interpretation of the meaning of an experience, which guides subsequent understanding, appreciation, and action. What we perceive and fail to perceive and what we think and fail to think are powerfully influenced by habits of expectation that constitute our frame of reference, that is, a set of assumptions that structure the way we interpret our experiences. (Mezirow, 1990, p. 1)

Critical reflection involves examining our own beliefs and views, with the following questions in mind:

- What underlying assumption or belief caused us to make a decision about a character or plan of action in a case study?

- Could those underlying assumptions be accurate or flawed?
- Could they be viewed differently by someone else?

Brookfield (1987) notes that "Thinking critically involves our recognizing the assumptions underlying our beliefs and behaviors. It means we can give justifications for our ideas and actions. Most important, perhaps, it means we try to judge the rationality of these justifications" (p. 13).

If we want to critically reflect on our own beliefs and assumptions, we must first be aware of those assumptions (Brookfield, 1987). How many of us are actually aware of the underlying beliefs and assumptions that we use to guide our problem solving and decision making on a daily basis? Most of the time, these views are so ingrained in us that we take them for granted; often not even considering them. Problem based learning activities such as case studies are important ways in which learners can reflect critically on their own beliefs and assumptions.

The process of critical reflection all sounds fairly straightforward, but in reality, it is not easy for people to do. The questioning of firmly established beliefs, values and assumptions can be a painful and difficult process. It requires the participant to be open to the possibility that their beliefs, values and assumptions are incorrect, narrow, or not applicable in every situation. It also requires the participant to be open to hearing the understandings of others. The result may be a stronger yet more flexible set of beliefs, values and assumptions, but it takes a lot of critical reflection to get to that point.

CRITICISMS OF THE CASE STUDY APPROACH

Case studies, like any other educational tool, have their share of limitations and criticisms. A major limitation is that case studies all require the student to make decisions based on a point in time. Unless they are written in sections, each of which is distributed after the prior section is analyzed, they cannot replicate the actual happening of events as they occur.

Occasionally, cases are written to include follow-up information, which the instructor may share with students after the case has been analyzed. Students can examine what was actually done in response to the issues described in the case study, but it is not a case of learning what the correct or incorrect response was. In fact, case studies may be difficult for students who are ultimately looking for right or wrong answers, as there typically are not right or wrong answers to case studies. Sometimes the actions taken by characters in the case study were less than effective. A student studying a case may develop an effective solution to the case, but because we cannot put that solution into actual play, we cannot tell if the

Ten Second Tip

As with all educational methods, case studies do have both critics and limitations in terms of their effectiveness in educational situations.

Figure 1.6.

solution is truly effective. Instructors can, however, grade student responses to case studies based on the thought processes used, the application of theory to practice, and the connections made to course topics.

Another limitation to the case study method is that the case study itself must be appropriate to the audience. A case study with too many details can result in students being overwhelmed, or not able to separate pertinent information from extraneous detail. This may cause students to shut down or become disinterested. This is also an issue if the case study is written at a level unsuitable for the audience. Case studies that are too difficult or too easy will not elicit the interest from students that is necessary for proper analysis. Remember that in effective analysis of case studies, students are required to actually place themselves in the case. This will not happen if students cannot relate to the case.

On the other extreme, the case study methodology has been criticized for providing students with too much information presented in a neat and orderly fashion (and thereby limiting students' ability to solve problems in real situations with less than perfect information). In response to this critique, some instructors are using abbreviated case studies with limited information presented. These types of case studies, called decision briefs, allow students to address problems with very limited information and incomplete data, with the purpose of preparing the student for decision making in these types of situations in the real world. Rather than a traditional case study narrative, students might view a video interview, and review some company documents that include some general information about the company and some specifics on the issue to be studied (Gloeckler, 2008). These objects would be examined in no particular order and with no predetermined prioritization.

SUMMARY

In order to most effectively use case studies as teaching tools, it is important to have some background information on them. This chapter has been an introduction to the use of case studies as teaching tools, and included definitions, types of case studies, and the history of the case study methodology. The theory behind the use of case studies, along with a discussion of problem-based approaches to learning, was also included. As is the case with any approach to learning, there are both positive and negative aspects to using case studies in the classroom. Both positive aspects and criticisms of the case study approach were included in this chapter. Consider how the information presented in this chapter will inform your use of case studies in the classroom.

REFERENCES

Armistead, C. (1984, February). How useful are case studies? *Training and Development Journal, 38*(2), 75-77.

Avillo, A. (2008). *Fireground strategies*. Tulsa, OK: PennWell.

Bandura, A., & Walters, R. H. (1963). *Social learning and personality development.* New York, NY: Holt, Rinehart & Winston.

Brookfield, S. D. (1987). *Developing critical thinkers: Challenging adults to explore alternative ways of thinking and acting.* San Francisco, CA: Jossey-Bass.

Campoy, R. (2005). *Case study analysis in the classroom: Becoming a reflective teacher.* Thousand Oaks, CA: Sage.

Ellet, W. (2007). *What is a case?* Boston, MA: Harvard Business School Press.

Erskine, J. A., Leenders, M. R., & Mauffette-Leenders, L. A. (1981). *Teaching with cases.* Waterloo, Canada: Davis and Henderson.

Ewing, J. (1999, November 15). Siemens: Building a "B-School' in its own back yard. *Business Week, 3655,* 109-110.

Gloeckler, G. (2008, February 4). *The case against case studies.* Retrieved from http://www.thefreelibrary.com/THE CASE AGAINST CASE STUDIES -a01611459479

Herreid, C. F. (2006). *Start with a story: The case method of teaching college science.* Arlington, VA: National Science Teachers Foundation Press.

Lockley, L. C. (1950). Notes on the history of marketing research. *The Journal of Marketing, 14* (5), 733-736.

Lundeberg, M., Levin, B. B., & Harrington, H. L. (1999). *Who learns what from cases and how? The research base for teaching and learning from cases.* Mahwah, NJ: Erlbaum.

Merriam, S., & Caffarella, R. (1999). *Learning in adulthood: A comprehensive guide.* San Francisco, CA: Jossey-Bass.

Merseth, K. K. (1991). The early history of case-based instruction: Insights for teacher education today. *Journal of Teacher Education, 42*(4), 243-249.

Mezirow, J. (1990). *Fostering critical reflection in adulthood.* San Francisco, CA: Jossey-Bass.

McKeachie, W., & Svinicki M. (2005). *Teaching tips: Strategies, research and theory for college and university teachers.* Belmont, CA: Wadsworth.

McNergney, R. F., Ducharme E. R., & Ducharme, M. K. (1999). *Educating for democracy. Case-method teaching and learning.* Mahwah, NJ: Erlbaum.

Norman, G. R., & Schmidt, H. G. (1992). The psychological basis of problem-based learning: A review of the evidence. *Academic Medicine, 67*(9), 557-565.

Von Glasserfeld, E. (1995). A constructivist approach to teaching. In L. Steffe & J. Gale (Eds.), *Constructivism in education* (pp. 17-39). Hillsdale, NJ: Erlbaum.

Wasserman, S. (1994, April). Using case studies to study teaching. *Phi Delta Kappan, 75*(8), 215.

CHAPTER 2

USING CASE STUDIES

Why use case studies in the classroom? Chapter 1 revealed that there are many benefits to using case studies as instructional tools. It presented reasons why instructors may want to use case studies as part of their overall teaching strategies. However, how those cases are used is equally important. This chapter deals with the "how" aspect of case studies used in education; or how to use case studies in the classroom.

Like anything else, case studies are not effective unless they're used correctly. The effective use of case studies depends on a variety of factors. The case study itself, the instructor, the learning goals, the educational environment, and the participants should all be considered when determining how to use a case study.

START WITH THE OBJECTIVES AND CONSIDER THE CASE

The case study should be seen as a natural activity that is within the guidelines of the course itself. Case studies used simply as filler in the classroom will result in lack of interest and confusion on the part of the students. Using irrelevant and inappropriate cases will also hinder the instructor's efforts to use cases in the future—even though those future case studies may be appropriate. For the case to be relevant, it is important that the instructor understand the objectives for the course and the purpose of the course in the overall curriculum. Those learning objectives should be clearly stated so everyone in the classroom is on the same page.

Case Studies and Activities in Adult Education and Human Resources Development
pp. 21–36
Copyright © 2010 by Information Age Publishing
All rights of reproduction in any form reserved.

	Ten Second Tip
	Before using a case study, instructors should consider the learning goals, the environment, and the participants.

Figure 2.1.

To clarify expectations for case study work in class, instructors should consider preparing some general guidelines for addressing case studies. Those guidelines might include information on how to effectively examine and participate in case study exercises. They may also include guidelines for effective discussion and case study critique. Consider the classroom environment when developing these guidelines. Guidelines for the use of case studies in distance learning environments would probably include different details than those for the traditional face-to-face classroom. Many suggestions for student guidelines can be gathered in the following sections of this chapter, where all of these issues are discussed.

Examine the Environment

The classroom environment is an important, yet often overlooked aspect of case-based learning. In order for the case study concept to be effective in the classroom, that classroom must be one that is conducive to adult learning. Remember that case-based learning is learner centered—not instructor centered. To be most effective, instructors using cases as instructional tools should understand the concept of andragogy, or the teaching of adult learners. Taking an andragogical approach when using case studies in the classroom allows the focus of the activity to be on the student, thereby maximizing the benefit of the approach. It also allows for greater student involvement and provides opportunities for students in the classroom to highlight and build upon their prior knowledge in relation to the case being studied.

Introduction to Andragogy.   A basic overview of the concept of andragogy is presented here. In the late 1960s, and based on European concepts of adult learning, Malcolm Knowles proposed the concept of andragogy, or "the art and science of helping adults learn" (Merriam, Caffarella, & Baumgartner, 2007, p. 84). Key in the concept of andragogy are several assumptions about adult learners. Adult learners, Knowles believed, are

	Ten Second Tip
	Understanding and implementing principles of andragogy will help create a classroom environment in which case studies are effective learning tools.

Figure 2.2.

self-directed. They collect experiences throughout their lives which they bring to each new learning situation. They are ready to learn when they perceive a need to learn, and are more problem-centered than subject-centered in their learning. Knowles also believed that adult learners are internally rather than externally motivated to learn, and that they need to understand why they need to learn something (Merriam et al., 2007). As opposed to the pedagogical approach, which is instructor-directed and formal in climate, andragogical approaches center on the learner and that learner's needs. Because those needs may be different for each learner in a classroom, the andragogical approach is flexible enough to allow for those different needs to be met, while still staying within a general framework of course topic.

The Andragogical Classroom.   How does an understanding of the concept of andragogy help facilitators of case-based learning? As you read the following section, consider the way the andragogical classroom is organized and managed, and consider how case studies can be effective tools in the andragogical classroom.

Here's what an andragogical classroom looks like: It features an environment of open communication and trust among the students and between students and facilitators.

- The focus is on the learner, and all activities are designed to center around the needs of the learner.
- The classroom atmosphere is informal, collaborative and supportive, and the instructor and the learner work together to determine that learner's needs.
- Based on those needs, the instructor and learner again collaborate on the setting of goals and the designing of methodologies to attain those goals.
- Activities in the andragogical classroom consist of learning projects, inquiry projects, independent study, and experimental techniques.

- There are no set steps to follow to get to the formal "end" of the lesson.
- Content is sequenced based on the needs and readiness of the learner.
- Learning activities could take the learner anywhere, and it is the instructor's job to support and guide the learner as they work through the learning process.
- Evaluation may be conducted by the teacher and the learner, but much of the evaluation is self-assessment on the part of the learner (Robinson, 1995). Andragogy also stresses the importance of each student's prior knowledge

and it is that knowledge, along with content learned in the classroom, that comprises the lens through which the student analyzes the case.

Based on this description of the andragogical classroom, you can see how activities like case studies are effective tools in the teaching of adult learners. It seems that the case study method is made specifically for the andragogical classroom. Problems with the method arise, however, when instructors take more of a pedagogical approach in the classroom. In those environments, case studies are less effective, as they focus less on the needs of the learner and feature more one-way, rather than two-way communication. Therefore, it is important that if you want your case studies to be effective, to shift your classroom practice to those based on principles of andragogy.

Participant Readiness

"Students provide most of the content of a case discussion. In fact, if they don't come to class well prepared, the case method will fail because the people responsible for making meaning from the case are not equipped to do so" (Ellet, 2007, p. 2). It is important that students are prepared to discuss case studies in class, regardless of whether that class takes place in a traditional classroom, online, or any combination. In order to participate effectively, students must know the details of the case ahead of time. Course content presented earlier might focus on theories to examine or hypotheses to critique. These theories or hypotheses might be used in analyzing and making decisions about the case, but they are separate from the case itself. Theories and hypotheses studied in class, along with the details of the case are the tools that students can use when working through the case.

Instructor Preparation

Much of this chapter focuses on the preparation and duties of the instructor in the facilitation of case studies. The case study approach is learner centered, but that does not mean that the instructor has less to do. The difference is that much of the work done by the instructor happens in the peripheral; much of it out of sight from the students themselves. The instructor's agenda includes duties related to the preparation of the case, the students, and the environment.

What To Do. The preparation of students can be managed in part by the instructor. Glover and Hower (1960) note that "Many students are tempted to read cases through quickly as a kind of story and then to engage in a rather haphazard, easygoing "bull session," so general and abstract as to be of little value" (p. 15). It is important that students understand the details of the case, and that they consider all of those details when making case-related decisions. The instructor must be prepared ahead of time to review the details of the case with the students, and to check for understanding as part of case prework.

On the other hand, the nature of a case study is that some facts are included and some are omitted. Students may complain that they could come to conclusions more efficiently if they had more information. The instructor can also help keep students on track by emphasizing what is known and encouraging exploration and decision-making based on the facts that are available. Instructors must also manage the difference between the stated facts of the case and students' evaluation or impressions of those facts. For example, the facts stated in a case may be "The use of a job aid increased performance levels by 40%." A student may argue that it would be impossible to increase performance by 40% simply by developing and implementing a job aid, but these types of speculations are not relevant to the case study. In these cases, the instructor should steer the conversation to relevant variables in the case that could be considered to address the student's question.

	Ten Second Tip
	Consider developing guidelines for case study participation so all students are clear on the instructor's expectations.

Figure 2.3.

What Not To Do.   Equally important in the facilitation of case studies is what the instructor should not do. It would be easy for the instructor to prepare questions for consideration that would guide the students down a certain path, or lead them to the "correct" answer. The word correct in the prior sentence is set apart in parentheses because in case studies, there typically are no correct answers. For this reason, instructors should not lead students to what the instructor deems the correct answer.

In the cases presented in this book, there are no clear-cut correct answers listed. There are key themes for discussion, and there may be questions to ponder, but as is the situation with many case studies, no answers of any sort are presented. In general, some case studies do present follow-up information on what the organization actually did when faced with the situation discussed in the case study. That follow-up information may appear in a subsequent chapter of the course textbook or in an instructor's edition of a course manual.

Students tend to like answers or solutions that are clear cut. They may read that follow-up information and conclude that they made the right decisions or chose the correct course of action if their decisions agreed with what was actually done (and subsequently, the wrong decisions if they disagreed with what was actually done). In these cases, it is the job of the instructor to point out that what was actually done by the organization may or may not have been the right or wrong thing to do. The important thing is that students examines the cases and build substantiating evidence for their decisions. That thought process, taking into account the variables discussed in the case and making conclusions based on what is known, is the crux of the case study method.

During the study of cases, instructors may hear opinions or viewpoints that are different than their own. Those viewpoints should not be discouraged, nor should viewpoints that the instructor might strongly agree with

	Ten Second Tip
	Rather than focus on correct or incorrect responses, case study facilitators should focus on helping participants to think through their responses and suggest consideration of alternatives or potential consequences—both positive and negative.

Figure 2.4.

be encouraged. In this way, the instructor puts him or herself more in the role of facilitator, and more on par with the students discussing the case.

Starting the Case. The instructor or facilitator should open the case with a broad, open-ended question. "What happened with XYZ Company in this case?" "Does anyone see any issues in this case?" These types of open-ended questions allow students to present their thoughts without any initial influence from the instructor. Instructors must understand that students approach case studies from different perspectives and take into consideration their different experiences. One student might focus on the learning piece of a case; another might focus on an issue of diversity. Some may focus on facts, and some on feelings. Some students may identify with characters in the case, and address the case study from the perspective of that character. Students may also respond based on what they believe the instructor wants to hear.

At this point is it important that the instructor understand that different approaches are normal in the case study method. They may be confusing or overwhelming to some students, who may find it easier to simply shut down than to study the many details of the case. In these situations, the instructor can use inquiry to gain consensus from the group about how to address the many details. It's possible that the suggestion to prioritize details could also help get students on track. The following sections of this chapter will specifically illustrate how to use these approaches.

Using Questions. The use of inquiry can be beneficial to the instructor in many case study-related situations:

- How can we work together on X and Y?
- How should we best deal with this detail when this other detail seems to stand in the way?
- How can we come to a consensus when we each disagree about these two factors?

It is surprising to see the degree of creative responses that students develop to these types of questions when prompted by the instructor. Instructors, too, can benefit from case study analysis in that they often learn about solutions they had never considered.

The use of inquiry serves another purpose in working through a case study. It is inevitable in classrooms that some students speak up more than others. Instructors can use the inquiry method to encourage participation by all students in class. In using questions such as those noted above, and in asking quieter students for their opinions, they are engaging all members of the class.

The job of the instructor also involves synthesizing major themes or tones noted by students. The instructor can summarize what's been said by pulling together different students' viewpoints. Contradictions can be summarized the same way. Sometimes, the instructor may introduce points that haven't been mentioned by the class or solutions that haven't been considered. In these cases, tone is critical. These points should be brought in as points to consider, and not in such a way that the students view the instructor's contribution as the "correct" one.

The instructor's tone is also important in responding to student questions during the process of studying the case. As instructors, we want to help students learn by providing them with the answers, but remember that the case study way of learning is different in that it is learner and problem centered. Rather than responding with an opinion or an answer, questions asked of the instructor can often be turned back into questions for the class. "I have some ideas, but what does the group think?" or "Does anyone have a comment on that question?" are ways of turning a question around. The instructor can also take prior comments made and fashion a response to a student question based on those comments.

The broader purpose behind the use of inquiry is to help the students develop their own solutions rather than look to the instructor for the correct answer. Remember that in studying cases, the goal is not for students to arrive at one correct answer. If they did, the learning that occurred would be of little help to them in the future, as case studies are typically so detailed that rarely would a student encounter the same situation in a different context. This concept can be difficult for students to understand, as it is different than how things work in the traditional classroom. Most students enter classrooms expecting that the instructor is the one with the knowledge or the answers, and it is their job (the students' job) to take in that knowledge. That is not the way the process works in classrooms in which case studies are used. Instructors can properly set the stage for using case studies by addressing the following points with their students:

- The focus of a case study should not be a right or wrong conclusion, as often there are no right or wrong answers. The focus should be on problem solving, evaluating alternatives, and deciding on an appropriate course of action. That course of action will probably be different for each student, and will depend on how that student prioritizes and evaluates.
- Depending on the students in the class, there may be important points of the case that go unnoticed and un-discussed, and obscure points that are highlighted. A viable solution for one student may be viewed as "incorrect" by another. While this may be irritating to some students, the way in which case studies are examined differently by each student in a classroom is very similar to the way actual problems faced by organizations are addressed. Therefore, building

greater tolerance and understanding of the multiple ways people address issues is a valuable skill in itself.

- Classroom discussions of case studies may end with points unsolved, issues scattered, and contradicting conclusions. This is typical of case study discussions, and is a result of the myriad of ways each student addresses a case. Tolerance for the fact that case study discussions will not be wrapped up neatly at the close of the class session is an important skill to gain from these learning experiences (and in many situations encountered in life itself). The instructor may provide follow-up information on what was actually done in the situation studied; however, as noted earlier, what was actually done should by no means be viewed as the "correct" response, with all other responses being incorrect. Instead, it can be viewed as satisfying curiosity in demonstrating one course of action. Remember that the course of action taken in an actual situation is based on the thoughts and knowledge of the decision makers, and may or may not have been the best way to go (Bailey, 1960).

- Because students enter a case study focused on different things, case study outcomes may run the gamut in terms of focus, solutions proposed, and conclusions made. Instructors must understand this fact when analyzing or grading written case studies. When grading or assessing student performance on case study assignments, instructors can examine a variety of things, including the following:

  o Students' decision-making processes in evaluating the case.
  o The connections made to course readings and overall educational program goals and objectives.
  o The ability to connect theory to practice.
  o The framing of the case through multiple perspectives.
  o The identification of novel approaches.
  o The ability to justify a chosen course of action.
  o The ability to use effective language and meaningful words.
  o The ability to discriminate between fact and opinion in the case study (Fuller, 1960).

An appropriate way to assess student performance on a case study is by using a rubric that includes some or all of the above components.

Case Studies as Tests. Case studies may be used as classroom assignments and in examinations as well. The bulleted list above consists of points to look for when grading cases. What also may be useful for both students and instructors is information on what constitutes a poor response to a case study. Fuller (1960) studied unsatisfactory responses to classroom case studies, and found some commonalities among students who failed. He noted that students who failed were typically not good writers, and used language that was "clumsy and ineffective" (p. 125). He also found that students who performed poorly on case study exams were not able to discriminate between facts stated in the case and opinions stated by characters in the case. Rather than make the distinction, they treated every statement as fact. They also made generalizations and focused on stereotypes about characters in the case rather than focus on specific actions ("The office manager is a control freak," for example).

Students who performed poorly on case study exams also focused on small and limited areas of the case, as well as limited alternatives that were overly simplistic in nature ("The solution is simple—the worker should be fired") rather than examining the case as a multifaceted and complex situation. Many poor solutions centered on authority ("The boss should exercise her authority and change things …") and the fixing of a problem rather than the improvement of a process or situation. However, despite their simplistic focus and responses, poor performers typically noted that there wasn't enough information presented to provide a quality analysis of the case (Fuller, 1960).

While the above points are useful in evaluating case studies as course work or tests, a student's performance on a classroom case study exercise may not be an indicator of how much that student ultimately learns from the case. As is the case with any kind of learning, actually learning from case studies happens at different times as well. Students may come away from the case study with immediate understanding of a concept previously foreign to them. On the other hand, they may consider the case study long after the course period is over, and the learning that results from the case study may not occur until then. In courses that feature many case studies, students may refer back to specific characters or incidents in older cases when discussing current cases. They may also be reminded of situations discussed in case studies when encountering similar situations in real life. These scenarios are all the more plausible when cases studied in the class-

Ten Second Tip

Some common themes have been found among students who fail to address case studies in an effective manner.

Figure 2.5.

room are examined by prepared students, managed correctly by the instructor and are facilitated in an environment conducive to open communication and learning.

Understand the Learner. The duties of the instructor in the preparation of students and in the facilitation of the case itself are based on several key considerations. Instructors must first have a good understanding of the students in the class. They must understand students' existing skills and needs in order to make the case relevant to the student. The use of learner biographies, in which learners examine their own material, social, and cultural influences on their learning processes, may be helpful both for students and instructors. Compiling a learner biography may help students to examine and better understand their frames of reference and observation. Learner biographies will also help instructors understand those frames in each of their students, which will better help them to meet student needs (Leibowitz, 2009). In fact, instructors may also want to complete their own learning biographies, as a way of examining their frames of reference. That biography could be shared with students, so they are better able to understand the instructor's frames of reference. In a course in which case will be studied, the development of learner biographies may be beneficial at the start of the course.

In summary, both the instructor and students should understand their roles in the case study exercise. There is more to facilitating a case study than simply distributing the case as a handout and hoping for the best. As noted throughout this chapter, proper preparation is key.

Case Studies and Distance Learning

The general guidelines for using case studies as educational tools in face to face and distance learning environments are fairly similar except for the preparation work associated with using case studies in distance learning environments. Whether the distance learning environment is synchronous (real time), or asynchronous is also a consideration.

	Ten Second Tip
	Facilitators of case studies are most effective when they understand the learners with whom they are working.

Figure 2.6.

Synchronous Online Environments.   Examples of synchronous learning environments include classrooms that use videoconferencing technology or computer programs that allow students to interact with the instructor and with each other in real time. Instructors may be physically present in a classroom, or by themselves, teaching to classes of students in several different classrooms. These types of classrooms allow for interactive audio and video communication in real time, and in that sense they are similar to the traditional face to face classroom. All students should be able to see their colleagues in different classrooms, as well as the instructor.

Using case studies in synchronous learning environments requires the instructor to engage students in each different classroom in an effective and efficient manner. "Instructors not experienced with synchronous teaching (via video teleconference technology) revealed that they often focus their attention only on the students physically present in the same classroom; resulting in the perception that the instructor is not interested in the learning process of the distant group of students" (Rybarczyk, 2007, p. 32). A difficulty in using case studies in distance environments is that the instructor cannot physically walk around each classroom to monitor conversations, highlight important points made, and respond to questions and comments that might be overheard. To address that issue, consider the use of a co-instructor or the designation of a facilitator at each remote site who can "share important aspects of the distance students' discussion, and who can capture the attention of the instructor if questions arise. Designating these advocates in each classroom of a distance-learning environment is important for keeping students on track, especially during case discussions of more controversial topics" (Rybarczyk, 2007, p. 32).

It is also a challenge in synchronous distance learning environments for the instructor to note subtleties in students' facial expressions or voice intonations. Instructors should be aware of these limitations and to compensate, should pay close attention to the body language and nonverbal cues that can be observed (Rybarczyk, 2007).

Ten Second Tip

Case studies can be used effectively in online learning environments, but the use of case studies requires the instructor to be aware of additional factors inherent in online learning.

Figure 2.7.

Asynchronous Learning Environments. Using case studies in asynchronous environments can also be effective, but poses its own set of challenges. Case studies can be examined in online discussion board-type forums, whereby students review the case and post their comments, which are, in turn, responded to by other students. As with all distance learning, preparation is important in the use of case studies as teaching tools online. The case study should relate to course content and students should understand the reason for its use. A major issue in the use of case studies in this type of environment is participation timing. In theory, an online discussion should be similar to a discussion held in a traditional classroom. Students present ideas and others add comments, critique those ideas, and offer alternatives. This can be done in the online environment, but it tends to happen much more slowly, as different students post at different times. However, if organized properly, and if the instructor is actively involved in the discussion, it can be just as effective as a face-to-face discussion.

Typically, a case study is assigned as an activity for a particular unit of the course. Students read the course materials for that particular unit so they are able to address the issues presented in the case. However, as in most classrooms, some students will post comments on the case study early in the unit, and frequently throughout the unit, while others will wait until the very last day to post their comments, and may not post any type of follow-up comments at all. The dilemma of participation among all students is similar to that faced by instructors in traditional face-to-face classrooms. Some students participate to a great extent and others sit in the back of the room and don't say a word. As a result, those who have posted early may have meaningful discussions with their colleagues on their postings, but those who post late may have no discussion at all.

While this issue of participation cannot be overcome in the online environment any more than it can be in the traditional classroom, there are ways to encourage participation by all students throughout the course of the unit. The use of deadlines throughout the unit helps students stay on track. For example, if a course unit runs for 10 days, the instructor may have students post their initial comments to the case study by the fifth day of class, and may ask them to respond to the comments of four or five of their colleagues by day seven. If case studies are used throughout the course, these types of interim deadlines should be fairly consistent so students are able to stay on track rather than become overwhelmed by deadlines that change with every unit.

Similar to the way an instructor walks around a traditional classroom and listens in on group discussion of cases, the online instructor should participate in the asynchronous discussion on a regular basis. The instructor should pose questions to students based on their comments, clarify issues when the student may be going off track, and highlight good comments and critiques made by students. While it is harder to solicit partici-pation among students who are less active on these types of discussion forums, instructors can use other methods, including e-mail targeted to quieter students, to encourage them to post their comments and partici-pate in the discussion. An e-mail message sent to a student might include the same types of questions the instructor would use when targeting a non-participator in the traditional classroom: "What do you think of XYZ Company's approach to ..."; or "If you were in this situation, where would you start to gather information?" These types of open-ended questions can be almost as effective in online environments as they are in traditional classrooms. However, the type of communication typically used in online environments may be less effective in soliciting participation. In the tradi-tional classroom, the student will most likely respond to the instructor's question in some way. However, it is easier for a student to ignore the instructor's e-mail attempt to include that student in online discussion simply by ignoring the request.

THE FACILITATOR

You might assume that the instructor always serves as facilitator in the dis-cussion of case studies. However, students, individually or in groups, can also be effective facilitators—both in the traditional classroom and in online learning environments. Giving students the opportunity to facili-tate a case study discussion means that those students will have to be very well prepared to respond to the comments and critiques presented by their colleagues. In order to successfully facilitate, they will have had to put a good deal of thought into the intricacies and details of case itself. This preparation helps students to work on their high-level thinking skills, as well as their facilitation and presentation skills. If students are to act as facilitators, guidelines for the expectations of student facilitators should be developed and provided to them. Those guidelines may be developed by the instructor, or possibly by the students themselves.

SUMMARY

This chapter has provided you with the tools necessary for using case studies as learning tools in the classroom. Key considerations for the use of case studies are prepared students and instructors, classroom environ-ments that model the principles of andragogy, and case studies that are relevant and interesting to the learner. Charles I. Gragg (1960) was a pro-fessor at Harvard Business School and an early proponent of the case study methodology. He summarizes his views on the power of the case study as a learning tool below.

> The case system, properly used, initiates students into the ways of independent thought and responsible judgment. It faces them with situations which are not hypothetical but real. It places them in an active role, open to criticism from all sides. It puts the burden of understanding and judgment upon them. It provides them with the occasion to deal constructively with their contemporaries and their elders. (And) it gives them stimulating opportunity to make contributions to learning. (Gragg, 1960, pp. 11-12)

This statement, written in 1960, is still accurate today. Fifty years later, the case study is still a commonly used and effective classroom tool. The cases themselves may have changed, and the disciplines that use case studies as classroom activities may have expanded. The classroom has changed too, and now case studies are as likely to be facilitated in online classrooms as they are in traditional ones. The basic premises are the same, however, as are the rules and guidelines for case study facilitation and participation. Properly facilitated, case studies can place students in active roles in the learning process. They can be used to encourage creative thinking and decision making. They can prepare students for real-world scenarios, in all their complexity and variability. Case studies come as close as possible to bringing the real world into the classroom.

REFERENCES

Bailey, J. C. (1960). A classroom evaluation of the case method. In K. R. Andrews (Ed.), *The case method of teaching human relations and administration* (pp. 35-45). Cambridge, MA: Harvard University Press.

Ellet, W. (2007). *What is a case?* Boston, MA: Harvard Business School Press.

Fuller, S. H. (1960). An unsatisfactory examination paper. In K. R. Andrews (Ed.), *The case method of teaching human relations and administration* (pp. 122-137). Cambridge, MA: Harvard University Press.

Glover, J. D., & Hower, R. M. (1960). Some comments on teaching by the case method. In K. R. Andrews (Ed.), *The case method of teaching human relations and administration* (pp. 13-24). Cambridge, MA: Harvard University Press.

Gragg, C. I. (1960). Because wisdom can't be told. In K. R. Andrews (Ed.) *The case method of teaching human relations and administration* (pp. 3-12). Cambridge, MA: Harvard University Press.

Leibowitz, B. (2009). What's inside the suitcase? An investigation into the powerful resources students and lecturers bring to teaching and learning. *Higher Education Research & Development, 28*(3), 261-274.

Merriam, S., Caffarella, R., & Baumgartner, L. (2007). *Learning in adulthood: A comprehensive guide.* San Francisco, CA: Jossey-Bass.

Robinson, R. D. (1994). *Helping adults learn and change.* West Bend, WI: Omni-book.

Rybarczyk, B. J. (2007). Tools of engagement: Using case studies in synchronous distance learning environments. *Journal of College Science Teaching, 37*(1), 31-33.

CHAPTER 3

CASE STUDIES AND ACTIVITIES

The case studies in this book are a mixture of the categories described by Simmons (1974, cited in Armistead, 1984) in chapter 1. However, the majority of them are situational case studies. These case studies are most often based on actual events or scenarios that combined a series of actual events. In some cases names have been changed and locations have been made more generic to protect the identities of the original case study subjects.

Authors who were asked to contribute to this book were given broad guidelines about the cases they would be contributing. They were asked to provide scenarios that could be examined from the standpoint of a case study. They were also asked to provide issues and questions for discussion.

Except where noted, each case is a stand-alone scenario and should be examined by itself. However, there are a few cases that are related to other cases in the book. One example is the Dalton City case, which deals with steps in the training program development process. This case study starts with general information presented in the Training Program Development section. Different aspects of that case are presented as four separate cases in the three subsequent sections—Needs Assessment, Program Planning, and Program Evaluation. It is important to read the Dalton City overview when working on any of the Dalton City cases. If you are working on one of the Dalton City cases, it is helpful, but not necessary, to read the others as well.

The categorization of these cases by subject was somewhat difficult, as many cases included in this book touch on more than one aspect of adult

37

Ten Second Tip

Although categorized by primary topic, many of the case studies and activities presented in this book fall under multiple categories. Keep this in mind when determining what case study to use. You may find the perfect case study in a section you didn't expect.

Figure 3.1.

education or human resource development. For example, there are two cases in the section entitled "The Adult Learner," yet most of the cases in this book involve adult learners in some way. Some of the cases in the section entitled "Community Education" are directly related to program planning. When reviewing these cases, do not limit yourself to those in the sections in which you are most directly interested. You may find cases that more appropriately meet your needs in other sections; therefore, browse the entire set of cases to make your best selections.

It's also important to note that questions associated with one case can be used on others. For example, discussion questions in two cases in the section on training program development ask participants how they might design training programs from several different perspectives, using humanistic, behavioral, constructivist, and social learning theories. This type of question could used in other case studies, as having students evaluate cases from these four perspectives could be valuable in many contexts.

Classroom activities were also solicited and gathered for inclusion in this book. Included are a variety of activities that can be used in both traditional face-to-face classrooms and online learning environments. Some of the activities presented can be modified to incorporate specific subjects beyond those noted in the book. For example, the "Future Back Vision" and "Table Buzz" activities are presented using HRD-related examples, but the concept behind the exercise can be used with other topics determined by the instructor.

The contributing authors and I invite you to explore the vast storehouse of case studies we have designed for your instructional and training use. We hope you will find them useful, and hope they inspire you to create your own original case studies as well.

REFERENCE

Armistead, C. (1984, February). How useful are case studies? *Training and Development Journal, 38*(2), 75-77.

Case Studies and Activities

ADULT BASIC EDUCATION/LITERACY

Case: The Surprise

Case: Mr. B's Story

Case: The Surprise

Betty Adams worked in the adult basic education division of Eastern Community College. She coordinated and taught courses in basic math, English, and reading, among other topics. Eastern Community College was located in a town of about 12,000 people in a rural part of a southern state. The town had suffered economically for some time, with the loss of jobs to foreign competitors as of late, as well as the decline in agricultural production and revenues. The community college in which Ms. Adams worked enrolled about 4,000 students. While the basic skills program was not a high priority in the community college overall, it was deemed an important aspect of the school, and was viewed as one way to help high school dropouts learn enough to pass their GED exams.

Recently, the state had been offering various incentives to attract new businesses to the area. Because of these incentives, a large manufacturing plant had committed to build a facility in the town. This plant provided products for the airline industry, and found the town to be an ideal location. Necessary to the company's strategy, however, was a large potential pool of workers who had basic reading and writing skills.

Responding to the needs of the manufacturing company, the community college put Ms. Adams in charge of a literacy program that could be offered to potential employees of the organization, as well as to members of the community in general. Ms. Adams was excited to be involved, and went to work immediately in the planning and organization of the program.

A few weeks into her work on this program, she heard from a local pastor, who was very well known and popular in the town. The pastor wanted to schedule an appointment with Ms. Adams to discuss her new program. Ms. Adams was thrilled that her program had the interest of such a major community figure, and she welcomed the meeting with the pastor. She envisioned multiple opportunities for the pastor to lend his support to the program. "I was excited that he could be a great role model for the value of literacy to these young students; many of whom have struggled with literacy issues all their lives," she said.

At the meeting, the pastor led the conversation with something that shocked Ms. Adams. He, himself, could not read. He memorized sermons and bible verses in order to fulfill his duties as pastor, and relied on a variety of strategies to hide his illiteracy from his parishioners. He had heard about the program Ms. Adams was developing, and the reason he wanted to meet with Ms. Adams was to inquire about what he, himself, might do in order to learn to read. Ms. Adams took a few minutes to gather her thoughts after what she'd just heard.

Discussion Questions:

1. If you were in Ms. Adams's place, how would you handle this request from the pastor? What types of questions would you have for the pastor?
2. If you were the pastor, what would you see as the ideal way for you to improve your reading skills in this situation?
3. How should the status of the pastor in the community be considered (if at all)?
4. What issues around confidentiality should be considered?
5. What principles of adult education are in play in this scenario?

Case prepared by Steven W. Schmidt, PhD, of East Carolina University in Greenville, NC, and Judy Hill, of Lenoir Community College in Kinston, NC.

Case: Mr. B's Story

Literacy Volunteers of Fletcher County (LVA-FC) was a newly formed organization aimed at helping adults acquire basic reading and writing skills. The organization operated on a shoestring budget, and because of their lack of resources, phone calls that came in after hours were forwarded on a rotating basis to members of the organization. One retired gentleman, Mac, always volunteered to answer phone calls over holidays because he didn't travel at those times.

On Christmas Eve, Mac received a phone call from the psychiatric ward at Fletcher Memorial Hospital about a man, Mr. B, who had admitted himself that day because he was so depressed, he felt he was suicidal. When he was asked by the doctor what was one thing he could do right away that would help him feel better, he had said to learn to read. Mac immediately said that he would come over and do an intake interview so Mr. B could be matched with tutor. Upon their meeting, Mac felt a connection with Mr. B and he assigned himself to be his volunteer.

Mr. B was among the youngest of 13 children and his family lived on a farm in a very rural area. He said that by the time he came along his parents were just tired. They had made sure that the older children did well in school, but Mr. B was allowed to just coast. By the time he got to the eighth grade, he was so far behind that he dropped out of school to work on the family farm. Mr. B's twin sister completed school and went on to graduate from college and became a school teacher.

Mr. B learned farming by working alongside his father and after he was married, he bought his own farm. He read at a second grade level, and he never developed the fine motor skills needed to write well. His wife was his reader and she paid the bills and wrote all the paychecks for the men who worked on the farm.

M. B had great math aptitude and he balanced his bank account in his head. When it came time to get a loan to buy seed and fertilizer for the new growing season, he would go to the local bank where they all knew him. Most farmers had an itemized written estimate of how much money they would need for the season, however, Mr. B would figure out how many acres he was going to plant in soybeans, corn and hay, compute in his head how much seed and fertilizer he needed for each crop, and total the amounts. At the bank, he had a reputation for being extremely accurate in his calculations, so when he told his estimate to the bankers, they would loan him the money. Mr. B received that kind of respect and trust from his community.

Mr. B was a successful farmer for many years and he and his wife raised four children on the farm. Then one day, his wife announced that she wanted out of the marriage and Mr. B's world began to slide out of control. Without the assistance of his wife, Mr. B had difficulty managing the farm. These difficulties were compounded by changing economic conditions that hurt smaller family farms like Mr. B's. After a while, Mr. B was not able to maintain the farm, and he had to sell it.

Mr. B then went to work at the Pitcher Wetherill textile mill in a neighboring county. His job entailed fixing large machinery. While Mr. B had a great mechanical ability, he couldn't read the repair manuals. When a piece of equipment didn't work, he would open the manual as if he were consulting it. He was always anxious that someone might realize that the pages in the manual didn't match the piece of equipment he was working on. Later, someone asked Mr. B if he was afraid that he would seriously ruin a piece of expensive machinery, he said very softly: "Every day."

Mr. B was successful in his job at the mill, but when the mill closed, he was left with no job and no skills. It was at this point that he became seriously depressed and eventually ended up on the psych ward on Christmas Eve.

Discussion Questions:

1. What can you learn from Mr. B's story about the ability of people with low basic skills levels to survive in today's world?
2. How is life different for those with low basic skill levels?
3. Look back 10, 20, or 30 years and consider what you can learn about the changing requirements for employment and about simply living in today's world as an adult with low basic skill levels.

Follow-Up Information:

After intensive tutoring, Mr. B completed the LVA program and enrolled in a GED class at a local community college. After several short term jobs, he was able to find stable employment at a manufacturing facility. His relationship with his tutor, Mac deepened into a strong friendship and later he was able to help Mac as his health began to fail.

Case prepared by Elizabeth Knott, Ed.D. of East Carolina University in Greenville, NC.

ADMINISTRATION OF ADULT EDUCATION PROGRAMS

Case: What's the Plan?

Case: Full Service Continuing Education Centers

Case: A Community of Learners

Case: What's the Plan?

The information technology (IT) unit at a state university manages all of the varied computing activities of the university campus community, including computer networking, campus websites, student computer labs, technical support, and graphic design. In order to accomplish such a diverse set of tasks, employees within the unit work in specialized groups and need different skills to complete their jobs.

The IT unit was asked by the administration to enhance its training and development process after a thorough campus review of their practices. The review identified as an issue the lack of a coordinated strategy for training and development for the staff in the unit. The IT unit had a good vision to foster growth at the various career stages of its employees, but did not have a well-designed plan for accomplishing its vision. Part of the problem was a lack of communication about training and development at all levels of the unit. Also, staff training was not keeping up with the rapidly changing IT environment, which hampered the ability of staff to meet changing IT needs on campus. Although the IT unit had used a number of strategies to assess the training needs of unit employees, including asking employees to request training in which they wished to participate, surveying employees, and discussing training at meetings, the unit was still experiencing challenges in assessing the training needs of their employees as they worked in the dynamic and interactive campus environment.

A small team, consisting of two trainers, the director of human resource development, and an outside adult learning and training consultant, was formed to develop a new approach to staff training and development in the IT unit. The new approach would need to address training needs in an employee's current position and development needs for employees' career advancement within the unit, as well as foster communication about the training and development process.

General Question:

1. Taking the role of the adult learning and training consultant in the team: How would you go about working with the other team members in this case?

Discussion Questions:

1. What steps would you suggest that the team use in the process for creating individual training and development for each employee?

A process of this nature could be linked to a performance planning process.

2. What data collection methods would you use to identify learning needs of IT professionals? How would you know that the process is conducive to the unit? What data analysis methods would you use to look at the findings from the data collection to determine priorities for training and development?

3. How would you communicate the findings across the unit? What plans would you create to maintain training and development and enhance communication about training within the unit?

4. How would you evaluate the impact of the work you have done with the team after it has been implemented for a period of time?

Case prepared by Simone C. O. Conceição, PhD, and Brian A. Altman, both of the University of Wisconsin-Milwaukee, in Milwaukee, WI.

Case: Full Service Continuing Education Centers

The Continuing Education Center (CEC) of Southeastern University was established in the late 1960s as an integral service aspect of the university's founding as one of the state's two land-grant institutions. The CEC is led by a director and team of 12 program specialists, more than 100 adjunct/part-time faculty (from main campus and the community at large), and more than 30 staff employees. The director has been with the CEC since its inception, first as a graduate intern in pursuit of a doctorate in higher education administration and rising through virtually every department to the director's position.

The director is known for being motivating and charismatic, effective in communication and organization, skilled in fiduciary management, and a leader in the community. The majority of the program specialists had been *hand-picked* by the director—carefully mentored for their successful positions. Campus faculty and community leaders who teach for the CEC recognize and protect the lucrative opportunities. That the director is nearing retirement is met with both sadness for the CEC's inevitable loss, but anticipation on the part of some who would see the center moved toward other strategic initiatives.

The CEC is responsible for all noncredit professional continuing education, contracted business and industry training, basic skills and literacy education, medical and health/safety education, and the certification and licensure training and education for state and local government personnel such as emergency, fire, and police departments. As online learning emerged, the CEC quickly and subtly negotiated the expectation that they could better market, coordinate, and manage the increasing distance education offerings of academic departments. Relatively new in the CEC's arsenal of educational offerings are a multitude of online continuing education modules and certificate programs offered to professionals in the entire region. They also offer a wide array of leisure studies, including language training, sports, technology, craft, and a vocational education that attracts significant numbers of community residents.

The center is located on 20 acres immediately adjacent to the main campus of Southeastern University, enjoying not only the advantage of being near campus resources, but benefitting from the associated culture, infrastructure, and academic environment as well. Other advantages of being closely associated with the large and well funded university include faculty and research expertise, athletic and sports resources, marketing and public relations campaigns, as well as graduate interns who find the venue advantageous for applied research and several full-time graduate assistants assigned to the CEC annually. In addition, the CEC also boasts its own full-service conference hotel, complete teleconferencing capacity, auditoriums, classroom and lab space, numerous conference rooms, and offices and state-of-the-art technology for all full-time personnel.

As a separate, but key component of a larger public university, the CEC had for years enjoyed limited state funding, primarily in terms of administrative salaries and maintenance of the physical plant and equipment. For the most part, however, they were expected to operate on a fee-paid basis, drawing income from the many profitable programs offered widely across the region. As state economies began to tighten and legislative funding reduced for public universities, the CEC became a primary target for financial scrutiny and increased centralization of administrative control. Academic departments began to consider how they might assume some of the profitable instruction, certification, and online modules now in the hands of the CEC. Spreadsheets were examined for the profitability of the conference hotel and associated functions of the CEC. And, given the fee-for-services mandate for most of their services, state legislators began to question the even minimal funding awarded the center out of state budgets. The university president and provost initiated measures to centralize and thereby more closely control the day-to-day activities and profitability of the Center for Continuing Studies.

Discussion Questions:

1. What factors might now influence the director's retirement decision?

2. What type of leader or manager should be recruited to replace the retiring director?

3. What might be the result of tighter centralization of the CEC? How will such centralization impact the profitability of the CEC?

4. How might the public or community image of the CEC be altered by these changes (if at all)?

Case prepared by Vivian W. Mott, PhD, of East Carolina University in Greenville, NC.

Case: A Community of Learners

Dr. Albert Wynne is an associate professor in the Department of English Language and Literature, and is also the director of an English as a Second Language (ESL) program for adults at a medium-size state university in the midwest. The ESL program provides intensive courses to international students, and upon program completion, these students typically apply for undergraduate or graduate programs at this university. In its recently approved strategic plan, the university increased its goal for international student enrollment from 50 to 500 within the next three years. All new international students had to enroll into this ESL program for at least one term to improve their English proficiency and get familiar with the U.S. academic environment.

The current ESL program served about 50 students and employed one full-time instructor and several graduate assistants (GAs), who were also full-time students completing their master's in the English Language and Literature Department. Albert was informed that in the upcoming fall semester, the number of students was expected to increase to approximately 150. He got approval to hire additional graduate assistants and also several full and part-time instructors. However, physical space at the university was at a premium, so he ran into some issues finding office and classroom space on campus.

The composition of program instructors for the upcoming fall semester, along with their office situations, was as follows:

- Because the GAs were full-time students, they had the least work load, lived on campus, and shared an office, located next to the ESL program main office, where each had a desk and a computer. They also had the least amount of experience teaching ESL to adults.
- The full-time instructors had completed their master's degrees and had years of experience teaching ESL to adults. They were provided their own individual offices, but due to office space problems, their offices were located on the other side of campus.
- Part-time instructors did not have offices yet. They were asked to use the campus library and other campus facilities to hold their office hours for the upcoming academic year.

ESL classes were taught all across campus. Albert was very concerned that the office space and the classrooms for his program were dispersed throughout campus. In addition, all of his instructors had different teaching experience, very few of them knew each other, and many were new to this ESL program. Albert was concerned about how to bring all the instructors and students together. Specifically, he considered the following:

- How could he create a community where the instructors could share their instructional practices?
- How could he create a community where the instructors could help each other solve classroom problems (e.g., cross-cultural issues and use of campus resources)?
- What practices should be implemented to help the instructors build informal relationships among each other?
- What practices should be implemented to help the instructors build relationships with students?
- How could he establish effective communication (a) between him and instructors and (b) among the instructors?

Albert knew that potlucks around holidays such as Christmas and Easter were not enough to address these issues. He hired an Associate Director whose primary responsibility was to address these issues and mentor instructors.

Discussion Questions:

1. If you were the newly hired associate director, how would you address each of Albert's concerns?
2. As the program grows up to 500 students, more instructors will need to be employed. What other issues would you anticipate?

Case prepared by Maria S. (Masha) Plakhotnik, of Florida International University in Miami, FL.

INSTRUCTIONAL STRATEGIES/INSTRUCTIONAL DESIGN

Case: Rural Home Care and Hospice

Case: How Will We Train Them?

Case: Teaching Extremely Bright Learners

Case: Rural Home Care and Hospice

Connie Smith is the director of information systems (DIS) at Rural Home Care and Hospice, Inc. She is a registered nurse with additional training in network administration. Connie has transitioned into the DIS role from clinical director, where she led interprofessional clinical care teams. Rural Home Care and Hospice, Inc. operates in a 23-county region of the state. Nine offices are distributed throughout the region to offer home health care services, hospice services, private duty services, and special programs services for personal care.

Rural Home Care and Hospice employees are very diverse in scope of practice ranging from doctoral-prepared physical therapists to personal care aides who have training at a vocational level. Corporate training for back safety, fire and emergency policy activities, driving safety, patient confidentiality, cardiopulmonary resuscitation (CPR), and other specified required training has been held on an annual basis in the clinical office. Training has typically been delivered using videos with clinical education staff facilitation. The education department consists of an office assistant and three nurses who work full-time to train all staff. The education department and the information system department are centrally located at the corporate office in Lanesville. The director of education reports to the vice president of human resources while the director of information systems reports to the vice president of finance.

A decision has been made by the board of directors of Rural Home Care and Hospice, Inc. to upgrade their operations. Currently, some nursing staff document patient records using laptops, however their programs are not integrated with billing or finance. The proposed system will integrate clinical, operational, and financial aspects of the company including all health professional documentation. The system will maintain personnel information and facilitate scheduling coordination. It differentiates various levels of personnel access to protect information and limit scope of authority. The system will require training of all clinical staff, with specific training based on discipline. All office staff will also have different screens of operation based on their job description and duties from scheduling to billing.

The time from proposed system set-up to "roll-out" for full clinical operations is 18 months. Connie Smith has been placed in charge of designing the educational plan of action in coordination with the director of the educational department (who has no technological skills).

The proposed system has some online training developed by the vendor that uses interactive video to demonstrate screen operations. However, the online training is generalized and not customized to Rural Home Care and Hospice. Further, most clinical employees work in the field, and only 54% of the workforce has high-speed Internet access at home. Clinical offices do not have ample computer stations to train a group of employees at a time. Policy and procedure manuals, which include screen shots, are available to distribute in each office. Nurses comprise 48% of the clinical staff with a mean age of 47, most with 2-year ADN degrees and limited computer skills.

General Question:

1. If you were in Connie's position, how would you go about planning for agency-wide education that has such a wide breadth of adult learners?

Discussion Questions:

1. What type of training needs would you expect to find in this situation? Consider the skill-based needs of the employees (both business skills and job-specific skills), as well as the technical, interpersonal, and behavioral needs.
2. How might Connie organize teams across professions and clinical offices to plan for training?
3. How might differentiation in training be prioritized by the agency teams?
4. What challenges might Connie encounter in the process of preparing such a large scope of training needs?
5. What resources will be needed to provide the needed training?
6. How does the organizational structure assist or hamper the potential training outcomes?

Case prepared by Annette Greer, EdD, of East Carolina University in Greenville, NC.

Case: How Will We Train Them?

Garrett Williams was the manager of a large rental car company branch at one of the busiest airports in the United States. The branch employed over 150 people, and was open 24 hours per day, 365 days per year. The airport had recently undergone a major redesign that involved the construction of a new terminal and the rearrangement of parking structures, new roads into and out of the airport, and the movement of all rental car company desks. Unfortunately for Garrett, what made the airport parking, check-in, and baggage claim processes more streamlined for customers resulted in more difficult processes for customers who were renting cars at the airport.

All of the process changes were set to take place in 1 month, with the grand opening of the new terminal. At that point, passengers flying into the airport would have to take a tram to the area where all rental car company desks were located. After checking in and getting their car assignments, they would take a shuttle to the parking lots. The procedure was a bit more streamlined for the rental company's executive-level customers, but even that had changed.

Garrett knew it was important that everyone on his staff be trained in how the new processes worked by the time the new terminal opened and all of the new procedures were put into place. His goal was to have all employees on his staff thoroughly understand the new procedures for renting cars from his company so they could continue to provide the highest level of customer service possible. He had approximately 1 month to make sure his staff knew the new processes and procedures. He knew training would be a challenge, given that it would be necessary for all employees on all shifts, and simply closing the rental car operation at his airport for training at any point would be impossible. Furthermore, the operation consisted of a mix of both full-time and part-time employees, so not all employees worked every day.

Discussion Questions:

1. If you were in Garrett's position, how would you deliver training on these new procedures to the staff?
2. What materials would you develop and how would they be presented?

Case prepared by Steven W. Schmidt, PhD, of East Carolina University in Greenville, NC.

Case: Teaching Extremely Bright Learners

A medical school at a large southern university faced a problem similar to many professional schools: although faculty was extremely well educated and experienced within their own disciplines, most had never taken even basic courses in adult learning. Most were simply teaching as they had been taught. Although this may work in some cases, it does not address a growing need in professional education: faculty who are trained to use effective teaching strategies that meet the needs of today's adult learners.

The medical school had been offering some professional development in adult learning as continuing medical education (CME), but CME was not the best solution to this problem for two reasons: (1) CME content typically focuses on a single skill or content area (such as a new procedure) rather than being focused on broad interdisciplinary concepts; and (2) the instructional design of most CME programs is lecture-driven and does not reflect the constructivist approach favored by adult learners.

The solution was for the school of medicine to partner with the college of education to develop a four-course certificate program that provided graduate-level adult education courses specifically designed for current and future healthcare faculty. Each of the four 3-credit-hour courses is taught for graduate credit that may also be applied to a master of education degree if the learner decides to pursue a degree. The certificate is awarded through the graduate school and is recognized as an academic credential. It may be counted toward promotion and tenure or may be listed on a resumé if a faculty member seeks employment elsewhere.

Only one course is offered each semester and the schedule rotates over 2 years to avoid an academic overload on working professionals, many of whom also have long clinic hours. Participants do not go through the program in formal cohorts because the learners (physicians, dentists, nurses, and graduate nursing students) often have professional responsibilities that force them to "stop out" for a semester. The courses use a blended learning model with two thirds of the sessions taught face-to-face to provide personal mentoring and face-to-face teaching practice and one third taught online to provide schedule flexibility. Learners are permitted two excused absences during a course to accommodate professional obligations such as conference presentations. Readings, worksheets, and other documents for all sessions are posted to the course website.

Despite this attention to detail, the course design was simple when compared to the instructional design necessary to produce a successful program. High-level learners such as MDs and PhDs in nursing or biochemistry are demanding learners and expect an immediate return on their investment of time. Every week must provide a usable skill or technique.

Because it is difficult to find instructors with credentials in both adult education and clinical healthcare, the course director for each course is joined by a physician or nurse educator for at least one third of the class sessions. The participation of a clinical educator ensures that the basics of adult education are realistically integrated with strategies for clinic-based instruction and bedside teaching. In addition, all courses are taught on the health sciences campus to accommodate the schedules of these faculty learners.

Each course in the program works toward a summative assessment event. In most courses, this is a large-scale project that addresses an actual campus-wide challenge or problem. For example, one group of students in a program evaluation course completed an in-depth evaluation of the pediatric externship, and another group completed an evaluation of the medical school's standardized patient program. Because the "students" are actually healthcare professionals, these evaluation reports serve as real assets to the programs involved. The programs evaluated would probably not have been able to assemble this level of expertise on their own, and would probably not have been able to support the cost. For these projects, the class divides into teams. Students select the team on which they will work and often that selection is based on their own expertise. To ensure new learning, the teams are responsible for sharing their strategies and outcomes with the class at large so all will learn the process. In several cases, students have asked to serve on two teams; one that will benefit from their expertise and one that will help them learn new skills.

Assessing extremely bright learners can be a delicate task because they are used to being recognized as "experts" rather than learners. Because standards are set high, the rubrics must include exquisite detail to guide learners toward that perfect performance they expect of themselves. It is often better to plan fewer graded events of more importance than many smaller graded events that may be perceived as "busy work." But, to avoid losing the benefits of formative assessment, ungraded events may be used to fill that need. In other words, for advanced learners it is better to guide them without grading them until they have reached the level where they feel comfortable being graded.

In interdisciplinary courses such as education research methods, some learners may have more expertise with a specific topic than does the instructor (e.g., a PhD in education will probably not win a statistics "duel" with a PhD in epidemiology). Applying a basic technique of adult education solves this problem: let the expert student serve as the instructor and the instructor serve as a facilitator. As long as this "instructor" role is shared by all students at some point during the course, it works very well.

The cost of such a program is calculated in faculty time, so it is important to acknowledge that teaching extremely bright learners may actually be more labor intensive than teaching a more typical population. When learners are highly motivated and engaged, they will shower the instructor with new materials and new ideas for projects. Again, the instructor must act as a facilitator to ensure that the instructional design for the course does not change mid-semester, thus causing problems for other learners who have carefully planned their time and participation.

An old saying in business is that a satisfied customer is the best advertisement. This also holds true with instructional programs! Success breeds success, and as long as the courses continue to evolve to meet current needs of the learners and the campus they serve, the program will grow.

General Questions:

1. How might this model be applied to other professional schools or colleges such as law or engineering?
2. What aspects of the model could be applied in a business environment?
3. What are the major differences between the role of "instructor" and the role of "facilitator"?
4. How does a faculty member know when to act as an instructor or a facilitator? What qualifications would you look for in the faculty who teach these courses?
5. What strategies might an institution/school adopt to ensure institutionalization of a program using this model?

Discussion Questions:

1. Why was the traditional CME professional development model not the best solution for this problem?
2. What specific instructional design techniques were applied in this adult learning model?
3. What were the greatest challenges presented in teaching these extremely bright learners? How were they overcome?
4. What tangible outcomes motivated learners to complete the program?

5. What basic principles of adult education were employed in the development and implementation of this program?

Case prepared by Karen H. Miller, PhD, and Ruth Greenberg, PhD, both of the University of Louisville, in Louisville, KY.

Community Education

Case: Teaching in a Museum

Case: Partnering for Success: Community Education in Action

Case: Retraining for New Opportunities

Case: Teaching in a Museum

Ralph, a retired engineer, is a tour guide at the Langley Art Museum in Iowa. Each Tuesday, he gives hour-long tours to locals, tourists, or anyone interested. The museum's permanent collection, the art that is always exhibited, features artists from the region. Since Ralph has lived his whole life in Langley, he appreciates the local scenes and likes that his hometown has its own museum, whose mission is to inspire the residents of Langley through the visual arts. He knows many personal stories about the artists and their families. Ralph's retirement 10 years ago from Langley's power company prompted him to enter into a volunteer role, and he chose the museum. He loves speaking to groups and educating them about an area he knows so much about. His tours are very informative. Ralph has a favorite route through the museum that he takes all tours, unless those galleries are too busy, which irks him.

Guided tours at the museum are unsupervised. While Ralph has never had a museum employee go on his tours, museum staff members have overheard him on tours talking about each painting in great details, for example, the type of paint used, the historical setting, and so on. His wealth of knowledge is impressive. He particularly enjoys explaining the origins of the works local to where he grew up and lived. His favorite is of the hill where he used to play as a child. Unbeknownst to Ralph, these same staffers have observed his tour goers shuffling their feet, looking around at objects not being discussed, having private conversations among themselves, and sometimes even ducking out to the restroom and not returning to the tour.

Samantha is the new curator at the Langley Art Museum. She is energetic and very interested in learning about tour goers—their needs, reason for visiting, and their interest in art. As curator, she is responsible for selecting what art is shown during special exhibits and making sure the guides are trained. Coming from Los Angeles, Langley seems provincial. A big reason Samantha took the position is because a couple times each year, the museum dedicates one gallery to host special temporary exhibits. The idea is that each time someone visits the art museum; there is something new to see. Deciding what gets shown in the special exhibit space is Samantha's opportunity to be creative and expose the people of Langley to art from around the world.

In preparation for the newest exhibit, Samantha emailed museum guides attaching pages of information on the artist and paintings, and asked guides to include the works on their regular tours. It seemed silly to her to be this explicit, because she knew the guides would be excited to incorporate the new exhibit in their tours. Samantha also suggested activities that could be done with tours in the gallery, such as allowing free time for tour goers to explore on their own for a few minutes and asking open-ended questions. She requested guides come see her if they had questions. A week later, the new exhibit, abstract art by a very politically active Irish painter, opened. The large untitled paintings are full of color and it is difficult to make out any particular shapes.

At home, Ralph read Samantha's email and deleted it without reading the attachments. At dinner, Ralph told his wife, "The curator wants me to show some abstract works from Ireland. This is the Langley Museum! I know why this museum was started. People come to see local art. I am a volunteer, and a good one. The museum cannot make me do it."

The following week, Ralph is wrapping up a tour to ladies from a local senior center. Like Ralph, these ladies are longtime residents of Langley. Samantha catches the tour goers as they are about to exit the museum and inquired, "What did you think of our special exhibit of paintings from Ireland!? Aren't they spectacular!?" The tour goers look confused and turn to their guide, Ralph, as if for clarification.

Discussion Questions:

1. What should Ralph do?
2. What should Samantha do as a museum employee responsible for training guides?
3. What suggestions would you give Samantha for how to train her volunteer workforce?
4. Are learning outcomes relevant in this setting?
5. What is the role of the tour guide?
6. What methods can Samantha employ to transform the guided tour experience at the Langley Art Museum?
7. Is Samantha asking too much of volunteers?

Case prepared by Amanda Neill of Pennsylvania State University Harrisburg, in Harrisburg, PA.

Case: Partnering for Success:
Community Education in Action

The small town of Martina had recently struck a deal with a large industrial farm equipment fabricator, Campo Ltd. To encourage Campo, Ltd. to choose Martina as the site for its new plant, the town partnered with the county and the state to offer tax incentives and training programs to provide the plant with qualified workers. The capital to support the tax incentives and training programs were procured through an economic stimulus grant offered by the federal government and managed by state agencies to support economic growth and development in rural counties. The amount of money provided by the grant for the community education training program was $400,000. This project will provide a great economic boost as well as an increase in morale for the community and citizens of Martina.

Carmen Britt, a continuing education specialist at the local community college in Martina, was charged with the responsibility of organizing community education programming to prepare citizens seeking employment for potential jobs with Campo, Ltd. The positions that will be available range from line work to accounting. Additionally, though Campo, Ltd. will be relocating some upper-level management employees to Martina, there will be a number of managerial positions for which local citizens can apply. The community education program Carmen is planning is multi-faceted and includes training focused on resume preparation and interviewing skills, as well as classes and training specifically related to skills necessary for different positions within the plant. Also included in the program is a public education campaign informing citizens about the new industry and employment opportunities and training initiatives.

Some of the classes and training opportunities will be offered on-site at the local community college, some at sites within the community, and some will be offered online. Money from the grant was allowed to be spent on salaries for the community education coordinator and staff; training materials, advertising of educational opportunities, and transportation to and from classes. A percentage was also to be earmarked for scholarships for students who needed community college basic education courses prior to engaging in skill specific training.

In addition to the grant funds, Campo, Ltd. decided to provide the community education initiative with $75,000 to use at the discretion of the initiative developer, Carmen. There were no stipulations attached to the disbursement of these funds, but Campo, Ltd. asked for a report explaining the impact of the utilization of the funds they provided. This made Carmen a little nervous as she was the only one responsible for determining how and when to spend the funds. She decided to establish an advisory board to help make decisions and provide feedback about the development, implementation and impact of the program.

General Question:

1. What steps or processes should Carmen and the advisory board follow to decide how to allocate the funds they have available?

Discussion Questions:

1. Imagine you are Carmen. Explain the main purpose of your community education initiative.
2. How would you prioritize the component of your initiative (with regard to both focus and funding)?
3. How might the funds provided by the grant and the funds provided by Campo, Ltd. be used in complementary ways?
4. What might be some of the challenges Carmen and her board may face in planning and implementing a comprehensive community education initiative?
5. Articulate any potential conflicts of interest that may present a challenge for Carmen and the advisory board.
6. How might Carmen assess the success of her community education initiative?
7. Describe a plan for assessing the impact of how the Campo-contributed funds were utilized and explain how you would present this information to the appropriate individuals at Campo, Ltd.
8. Beyond the primary purpose of preparing citizens for potential employment with Campo, Ltd., what impact might Carmen's program have on the community of Martina?

Case prepared by Kaye B. Dotson, EdD, and Kylie Dotson-Blake, PhD, both of East Carolina University in Greenville, NC.

Case: Retraining for New Opportunities

Raquel Mendez, an agriculture extension agent, had observed a trend in her community in recent years. As tobacco allotments dried up and the price of farm chemicals and fuel continued to rise, many small farmers were having difficulty making ends meet and had begun to seek other forms of employment, leaving farms fallow. Many acres of prime farm land had become covered in weeds and there was a sense of dejection in the small, rural community. Raquel's community has a population of less than 20,000 with 26% of the population living beneath the poverty line. The agriculture and timber industries were primary employers for workers in the county, along with state and local government agencies. However, with many of the farms being removed from the commerce chain, county citizens were having a great deal of difficulty finding employment.

Unfortunately, with only one high school and a partnership that provided limited community college education opportunities through the satellite campus of a neighboring county's community college, there were few retraining programs for displaced farmers and farm workers. At the same time, Raquel had been receiving many calls from local restaurant and grocery owners asking for information about purchasing local produce, as the costs for shipping produce in from external sources had risen along with fuel prices. Most of the local farmers did not grow produce beyond small amounts for their individual families and Raquel had not been able to offer any solutions to the local restaurant and grocery store owners.

As Raquel puzzled these issues over in her mind, she began to develop a vision for addressing these related concerns through an innovative new program. The program she envisioned would encourage local farmers to shift their focus from externally marketed goods, such as soybeans, tobacco and cotton, to food items that local restaurants and grocery stores could purchase for sale to local citizens. Her program has the potential to meet the needs of farmers and farm workers to make a profit from their land while meeting the needs of local restaurants and grocery stores for affordable, fresh produce. However, switching from the crops they had formerly grown would require that farmers modify equipment, receive training on how to effectively grow new crops, and learn what chemical treatments are allowed by the FDA for local produce intended for sale to groceries and restaurants for human consumption.

Raquel's history of engagement with the local farm community helped convince her that to implement this new program, she would need to rely on leaders in the community to promote the necessary education opportunities and benefits of working together to bring the program to fruition. With this in mind, she began the program planning process by contacting local community leaders with ties to the farm community. She set up a series of meetings to assess community support for the program and began developing collaborative team to work on planning and implementing the program.

From her meetings with the community leaders, Raquel gained the needed support for her initiative, but also received valuable feedback to better position her program for success with the farm and business communities. During the meetings, Raquel and the leaders decided that a needs assessment should be conducted with local restaurants, inns and groceries to determine the types and quantities of produce they may potentially purchase locally. The group decided that this needs assessment should extend to neighboring counties to broaden the potential market for farmers who decide to transition to the new program. Additionally, the group advised Raquel to work with the local chamber of commerce to determine if any state or federal grants existed to support retraining and retooling efforts required by Raquel's new program.

Raquel decided to work with other agricultural extension agencies to determine if programs for retraining existed to help farmers learn processes and regulations associated with running produce farms. Finally, the group and Raquel decided that community education would be one of the most important components of the program, as it would help to boost sales of local produce within the community, increase the participation of farmers, and provide visibility to the initiative.

General Question:

1. In considering the community education initiative, what, if any, are the most significant components that Raquel might choose to include?

Discussion Questions:

1. How might Raquel assess the impact of her community education initiative?
2. What stakeholders might Raquel target with this component of her program?
3. How might Raquel promote the benefits of her program through the community education initiative?
4. What, if any cultural challenges, do you think Raquel might encounter in trying to implement her innovative program with farmers and business owners in her county?

Case prepared by Kylie Dotson-Blake, PhD, and J. Scott Glass, PhD, both of East Carolina University in Greenville, NC.

TRAINING PROGRAM DEVELOPMENT

Activity: Training the Trainer

Activity: Up to the Job

Information: Dalton City Overview

Activity: Training the Trainer

Introduction:

A very important skill in the field of adult education and training is to be able to design and develop educational programs from multiple perspectives. Merriam, Caffarella, and Baumgartner (2007) compare and contrast the behavioral, humanistic, social, cognitive, and constructivist learning orientations. The following case is designed to assist you in developing skills in designing adult education and training programs from these varied perspectives.

The Case:

You are employed at the corporate level by a pharmaceutical company who is preparing to release a new product. Because this new product is very complex, you know that a great deal of training will be needed for the sales staff to effectively explain this product to the physician customers. You decide that you would like to train a group of 30 trainers from four different areas of the country to educate the sales staff on this new product. The trainers will need to know the new product, but will also need to understand how to train the sales force in their region. These trainers are new hires for the organization. Your role is not one of training the sales force, but rather training the trainers to work with the sales force.

Discussion Questions:

1. How would you develop this training program from a humanistic perspective?

   Outline the following for your program:

   - Needs assessment
   - Program design
   - Program objectives
   - Learning activities
   - Evaluation strategies

2. How would you develop this training program from a behavioral perspective?

Outline the following for your program:

- Needs assessment
- Program design
- Program objectives
- Learning activities
- Evaluation strategies

3. How would you develop this training program from a constructivist perspective?

Outline the following for your program:

- Needs assessment
- Program design
- Program objectives
- Learning activities
- Evaluation strategies

4. How would you develop this training program from a social learning perspective?

Outline the following for your program:

- Needs assessment
- Program design
- Program objectives
- Learning activities
- Evaluation strategies

REFERENCE

Merriam, S. B., Caffarella, R. S., & Baumgartner, L. (2007). *Learning in adulthood* (3rd ed.). San Francisco, CA: Jossey-Bass.

Activity prepared by Barbara J. Daley, PhD, of the University of Wisconsin– Milwaukee, in Milwaukee, WI.

Activity: Up to the Job

Introduction:

A very important skill in the field of adult education and training is to be able to design and develop educational programs from multiple perspectives. Merriam, Caffarella, and Baumgartner (2007) compare and contrast the behavioral, humanistic, social, cognitive, and constructivist learning orientations. The following case is designed to assist you in developing skills in designing adult education and training programs from these varied perspectives.

The Case:

You are working at a large, urban community college as an adult educator in a GED preparation program. Your college has just received a major contract with a local employer to train 55 people for entry level employment at a food packaging warehouse. As the city has felt the effects of recent economic downturns, the addition of staff at the food packaging warehouse, which was located in an industrial area near the city's downtown, was met with great response from community leaders. Leaders at the community college were also excited to be partnering with the food packaging organization.

Employees to be hired by the food packaging company will be working on the line packing a variety of food products. The company feels they can handle the specific training related to packaging of food products, but has contracted with the community college to develop a program to increase the literacy skills of the workers hired and to assist in creating workers who are responsible, punctual, and loyal. The company feels that adding literacy skills to the training program could potentially assist with worker retention and loyalty. The company would like to decrease their turnover rate in these jobs and also make sure that the new employees can read and understand the training they will provide for the food packaging part of the program.

Discussion Questions:

1. How would you develop this training program from a humanistic perspective?

    Outline the following for your program:

- Needs assessment
- Program design
- Program objectives
- Learning activities
- Evaluation strategies

2. How would you develop this training program from a behavioral perspective?

   Outline the following for your program:

   - Needs assessment
   - Program design
   - Program objectives
   - Learning activities
   - Evaluation strategies

3. How would you develop this training program from a constructivist perspective?

   Outline the following for your program:

   - Needs assessment
   - Program design
   - Program objectives
   - Learning activities
   - Evaluation strategies

4. How would you develop this training program from a social learning perspective?

   Outline the following for your program:

   - Needs assessment
   - Program design
   - Program objectives
   - Learning activities
   - Evaluation strategies

REFERENCE

Merriam, S. B., Caffarella, R. S., & Baumgartner, L. (2007). *Learning in adulthood* (3rd ed.). San Francisco, CA: Jossey-Bass.

Activity prepared by Barbara J. Daley, PhD, of the University of Wisconsin–Milwaukee, in Milwaukee, WI.

Information: Dalton City Overview

Following is background information for a case that is presented in the next three sections of this book (Needs Assessment, Program Planning, and Program Evaluation). This case is designed to build upon itself, so please review this information before addressing the Dalton City—Needs Assessment Case. Review this information and the Dalton City—Needs Assessment Case before addressing the Dalton City—Program Planning Case, and review the Dalton City background information, needs assessment, and program planning cases before addressing the Dalton City—Program Evaluation Case.

Dalton City Background

Dalton City, NC, with a population close to 60,000, is in an under-developed part of the state. The region has traditionally been rural and agriculture has provided the primary economic base. But farming has been in a slow decline because of the disappearance of small family farms and the rising costs of farming.

Dalton City has been fortunate in the last 15 years with the relocation or expansion of several industries, including a major manufacturing facility for a large German medical equipment company. The city's population has grown dramatically and it has become more diverse with an increasing Hispanic population and the influx of people attracted to the growing manufacturing base. It is anticipated that Dalton City will be one of the few cities in the region to experience major growth in the future.

In addition to the growing manufacturing sector, the medical community has also expanded. The hospital in Dalton City has now become a satellite hospital for a large state medical school. This means that they now provide rotations for medical students and can accept residents. Accompanying this new development has been the relocation of some medical school faculty and the creation of new jobs in all of the allied health areas. There is also a small private college in Dalton City that has responded to the need for well prepared health professionals by creating numerous new degree programs such as medical technology, occupational therapy, and so on.

In response to these demographic changes, the local government has grown dramatically over the past 10 years. Like the city's other service organizations, city government has become greatly overextended in meeting the growing needs of city residents. This means that new positions are being created as fast as financially possible and reorganizations have become a way of life. In the past the organization has relied on human resources to provide general orientation for new employees and lower level supervisors to provide on the job training. It has also used external vendors to meet administrative or specialized training needs.

Information prepared by Elizabeth S. Knott, EdD, of East Carolina University in Greenville, NC.

NEEDS ASSESSMENT

Case: Dalton City—Training Needs

Case: Run Like the Wind

Case: Dalton City—Training Needs

Items to review: Dalton City Overview

Carol had retired from the Marines with 20 years of experience, the last 8 of which were as a trainer of maintenance workers for heavy transport vehicles and then as an instructor training and certifying future trainers. Because of this experience and because of her solid confidence and high energy level, Carol was hired as the first trainer for the Dalton City local government. When she came for her interview, it was clear to Carol that the local government was greatly in need of a centralized and coordinated training office, but she wasn't sure that they were even aware of how fragmented their training efforts were. Carol was originally from this region of the state so she was familiar with its agricultural tradition and the proud nature of its people.

City government had been growing very quickly as of late. Top city management realized that the approach they had taken to that point; having each supervisor responsible for the training of his or her employees, was leading to an inconsistent quality of training. They believed this inconsistency contributed to low job performance and possible job errors. In some areas such as law enforcement, street maintenance, and trash pick-up, job errors can have serious consequences like legal liability or bodily harm. Top management had also decided they wanted to develop a more cohesive organizational culture beginning with a focus on customer service since the citizens of the City were the "customers" to whom they provided services.

Another concern was the training of first-line supervisors for street and city infrastructure maintenance and repair. These supervisors are most often promoted from within a work crew and they may even be asked to supervise the same employees that they worked beside before their promotions. Because the educational levels of these employees are much lower than those in middle and upper management, prior opportunities for supervisory training are almost nonexistent.

Discussion Questions:

1. If you were in Carol's position, how would you go about learning about this organization's training needs (and what actions would you take to learn about those needs)? What might some of those needs be?

2.   How would you prioritize the city's training needs?

Case prepared by Elizabeth S. Knott, EdD, of East Carolina University in Grenville, NC.

Case: Run Like the Wind

Vicki Glenn had just accepted a position as training coordinator for the dealer service department at Arctic Wind corporation, a manufacturer of snowmobiles and related products, including replacement parts, accessories, and clothing. The 40 employees in the dealer service department worked in a call center-type environment that provided service for Arctic Wind's 500 retail dealers in the United States and Canada. They did not work with retail customers, and directed calls from those customers to Arctic Wind's customer service department. While all Arctic Wind dealers ordered all products electronically, via computer, the dealer service department provided information to dealers via telephone, e-mail, and instant messaging on product availability, specifications, order lead times, warranty coverage, and a variety of other topics. They also processed returns and remedied shipping-related issues. The employees in this department worked with many other departments in the organization to find answers to dealers' questions and to solve their problems. They also worked with a variety of external vendors that made products for Arctic Wind dealers. The department was managed by one supervisor, who reported to the director of sales. That director reported to the vice president of the sales department.

The dealer service department at Arctic Wind was a busy one, where employees worked at a fast pace. The department's mission was to provide superior service to Arctic Wind dealers, and to provide that service in a prompt and efficient manner. The department had grown large enough in the past few years to require the resources of a full-time trainer who would focus solely on the training needs of both new and tenured employees in the department. In her job interview with the departmental supervisor, Vicki learned that new employee training was considered a priority by upper management. Vicki was excited about her new job, and decided to start with an assessment of training needs.

General Question:

1. If you were in Vicki's position, how would you go about conducting a training needs assessment in this case?

Discussion Questions:

1. What type of training needs would you expect to find in this situation? Consider the skill-based needs of the employees (both busi-

ness skills and job-specific skills), as well as the interpersonal or behavioral needs.

2. What stakeholders might Vicki contact in order to determine the training needs for this department?
3. How might the needs that Vicki discovers be prioritized?
4. What hurdles or roadblocks might Vicki encounter in the process of gathering and prioritizing training needs?

Case prepared by Steven W. Schmidt, PhD, of East Carolina University in Greenville, NC.

PROGRAM PLANNING

Case: Dalton City—Program Planning

Case: Who Has the Power? (International Scope)

Case: Sid Simmons

Case: Program Planning at Harper Bank

Case: Dalton City—Program Planning

Items to review: Dalton City Overview
                    Dalton City Needs Assessment Case Study

Carol had learned the hard way from her experience in the Marines that it's too easy to lose some trainer credibility if, as a trainer, you don't understand or can't relate to the specific jobs your trainees do. She knew that to really understand the work, she needed to see them do their jobs in the actual context and under the real conditions that the jobs are actually done. During her first 3 weeks, Carol made contacts within each city division and spent time with the people who actually did the work in that division, including the following:

- riding with a sanitation crew on its daily trash route;
- following an animal control officer for a day;
- sitting behind a desk and answering the phone in the tax office;
- working with someone from parks and recreation responsible for the scheduling and maintenance of one of the city's large parks;
- working with a crew in fleet maintenance for a day;
- spending a day in the clerk of court office observing and interviewing employees; and
- shadowing someone from code enforcement as he made his rounds.

These visits also served a second purpose for Carol. Not only could she learn about the work the City does, but she could make valuable contacts within the management in each division and begin to get a feel for any possible needs that might emerge from these discussions. Also, once she was further established in her job, Carol hoped to develop a training advisory board. The networking involved in visiting the divisions and meeting employees would be helpful in forming that group.

In her job interview, the top management team kept stressing the need for customer service training and training for new first-line supervisors. Carol knew that was the place for her to begin in developing new training programs. She also felt that being able to produce tangible and credible programs early on would establish her in the job and reassure the management team that they had made the right choice in hiring her. Therefore, while she was learning about the organization through meeting with various folks, she also started working on her first programs.

After reviewing several packaged customer service training programs, Carol decided to create her own program to fit the format suggested by top management: 6 hours of training scheduled in 2-hour sessions over 3 weeks. Because of the heavy workloads that most employees carried, they were concerned that job efficiency might suffer if employees were pulled from their jobs for a longer period of time.

Carol was pleased that management had supported her suggestion that *all* city employees receive this customer service training. If management wanted to create a service-oriented culture across the organization, Carol felt it was critical that *every* employee understand the concepts of customer service and how they applied in his or her own job.

For the first line supervisor training, Carol decided to purchase a popular vendor-prepared supervisory training program. While the City would have to pay for the basic training materials from this private vendor, the materials were reasonably priced, had been widely used, and were proven to be effective. In her decision making, Carol had also consulted with several other local government trainers that she had met through regional meetings of a training and development association about the types of first line supervisor training that they provided. Several of these trainers highly recommended this particular program.

Discussion Questions:

1. If you were in Carol's position, how would you design a customer service training program for all city government employees? From what stakeholders might you get input? Where might you find resources for this course? What would the program look like? What is the best way to deliver this program?

2. What are the advantages and disadvantages of Carol's purchasing a vendor-prepared supervisory training program and of her developing the customer service training program on her own?

3. What considerations specific to the city would be important to remember when designing the customer service program or when customizing the supervisory training program specifically for the city?

Case prepared by Elizabeth S. Knott, PhD, of East Carolina University in Greenville, NC.

Case: Who Has the Power?
(Program Planning in an International Context)

Several years ago, SHU University in China provided a training program for leaders from the national electric power industry in China. This leadership training program was regarded as a window through which the university could enlarge its network with the electric power institutions and was therefore given high priority and much attention in the university.

The program lasted for 3 months. The three planners were: Wu, the director of the training center, who was responsible for the strategic planning and the key negotiations; Zhu, the director of the program, who was responsible for planning the whole program; and Liu, who was a new employee brought on to assist with Zhu's work.

The competition in the leadership training market had become fierce in China in recent years. SHU had a good relationship with the electric power industry, and a good reputation for training as well. After countless contacts, the Training Center of SHU signed the contracts with three big companies to train their leaders from a combined five provinces and 17 cities about the new management practices and China's market-oriented consciousness.

Three planners collected the basic demographic information from these leaders. The feedback showed that 65% of them were from Northwest China, a comparatively poorer economic area; 13% were from East China, a comparatively richer economic area; and 22% were from Shandong province in North China, which has a high economic level. There were 3 females and 2 minorities. Their average age was around 40.

From the conversations, the planners knew that most of the leaders preferred to have more informal activities, such as investigating and visiting the well-known enterprises, traveling, sightseeing, and having parties and social events. They indicated that they had had several such management trainings. They were very busy and tired in their routine work and wanted more time to relax, and at the same time make friends and enlarge their networks with colleagues at other electric power companies. Learning about management in a formal classroom was of little interest to them.

The companies involved would pay for the programs, and learners would evaluate the training at the end of the program. Zhu made a plan to balance the needs of both the learners and the companies: two-thirds time spent on face-to-face courses, and one-third time on informal activities, including one international trip to Russia, two long-distance trips to south China, and four short-distance trips to nearby Shanghai on the weekends; three visits to well-known enterprises in Shanghai; and also weekend parties. At the first stage, the learners would have intensive study and short-distance trips; at the second stage, less intensive study, long-distance trips and visits to the enterprises; at the third stage, loose study, written tests, and travel to Russia. In addition, Zhu scheduled one party per week.

In designing this initial draft, two issues were highlighted: budget and instructors. Considering 65% of the leaders were from the northwest with comparatively poorer economic condition, the center charged lower tuitions (in comparison with market prices). To make profit from this program, Zhu used many strategies. For example, she asked two leaders from East China if they could sponsor two short-distance trips in their regions. Through negotiations, these two leaders successfully persuaded their local government leaders to sponsor these two trips. Hotel budgets were also carefully planned to cater to the different stakeholders' abilities to pay. In the previous programs, many attendees complained about the poor conditions of the SHU hotel, although it was cheaper than the hotel outside the university. In this program, Zhu still recommended the learners use the SHU university hotel since the university wanted to make money from the program and the companies paying for the training expenses wanted to save money.

The instructors were mainly from universities, government, and companies. In previous programs, nearly every learner was dissatisfied with one instructor named Hu, a powerful leader of the SHU University. Although Hu had recently transferred to another university, Wu and Zhu still employed him in this program, as they were concerned that his power networks were still in place at SHU. Zhu said: "I am only a program director, I need to make a living, and I do not want to lose my job." Liu was concerned that with Hu as an instructor, the training center would lose clients. Zhu agreed: "I know. We need to think of alternative ways to have the university get rid of him, maybe through learners' evaluations."

In the initial planning draft, Zhu listed a full service plan for attendees, even addressing issues of diversity such as offering a kitchen for two Muslim minorities. At the same time, she negotiated with different organizations involved: restaurants, gift factories, places of entertainment, tour agencies, and so on. After endless negotiations and comparing different prices and services, the training center and some of these organizations achieved oral agreements on service and discounts.

The program was successful in terms of developing good relationships with the attendees. The 3-month program broadened the attendees' knowledge and helped them to build trust and friendships among learners and planners. Attendees said the development of friendships among classmates was the most valuable aspect of the program, and they looked forward to collaborating with classmates on future business. They also expressed an interest in helping the program planners in the future. Most were fine with the living conditions at the hotel. Some of them actually found campus life to be interesting.

At the graduation ceremony, the main leaders from the university were invited. A video with highlights of the program was played, which was very popular. Wu's humorous and lyrical style narration of the program made everyone laugh, including the university leaders who seldom laugh on formal occasions.

On that evening, a big banquet was organized. Besides the learners and the leaders of SHU University, the main university staff from the financial department, logistics department, hotel, and personnel departments were also invited. Inviting them could be beneficial the next time we look for help with our programs, Zhu thought. Final program evaluations showed that some learners were not satisfied with some instructors and planners, and Hu was regarded as the worst.

Discussion Questions:

1. Table 3.1 shows different stakeholders' interests. What are the main interests of the different stakeholders?
2. How did the planners balance these different interests in this program planning process?
3. If you were a planner, how would you design this program to satisfy the different stakeholders' interests?
4. Figure 3.2 is a representation of the primary stakeholders' main interests. What would happen if the planners in this program overemphasized the political goals, social goals, or the educational goals and neglect the other goals?

Table 3.1.   Different Stakeholders' Interests

Stakeholders' Interest	Political Goals	Economic Goals	Social Goals	Educational Goals
Companies				
Universities				
Learners				
Planners				
Other organizations				

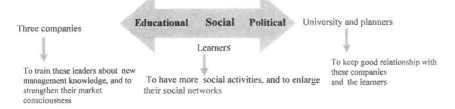

Three companies

To train these leaders about new
management knowledge, and to
strengthen their market
consciousness

To have more social activities, and to enlarge
their social networks

University and planners

To keep good relationship with
these companies
and the learners

Figure 3.2.   Main stakeholders' main interests.

Case prepared by Bo Chang, of the University of Georgia in Athens, GA.

Case: Sid Simmons

Sid Simmons works for one of the largest for-profit advertising/public relations firms in the world as the global human resource (HR) information systems support manager. Headquartered in Chicago, Illinois, the firm has 96 offices in 25 different markets around the world.

Sid has a bachelor of communication undergraduate degree with a focus in organizational communication. He also has a master's degree in human relations with a focus in organizational change and development. Sid was born and raised in Holland and at age 16 his parents moved to the United States. He started work as a trainer right out of college, training student volunteers to help the admissions office recruit potential students to the university.

He moved into the telecom arena as a training coordinator for a multinational corporation headquartered in Canada. Working with HR offices in 15 countries, Sid negotiated training contracts with vendors doing highly specialized technical IT training for developers. He was responsible for all aspects of training including logistical coordination of equipment, supplies, enrollments, tracking enrollments, and paying vendor invoices. Sid was promoted to training manager and responsible for the training for 1,300 IT professionals representing highly diverse backgrounds including Indian, Arab, Asian, and Middle Eastern. While at the telecom company Sid learned that the primary language in the company was French, with English being second. All training materials had to be written in French first and then English. Throughout his tenure at the firm he worked with the chief information officers of four business units to strategically coordinate what technology to introduce in IT and how to train the people in IT. A lot of the training had to do with large-scale systems implementations.

When the human resource information systems support manager position opened up at the advertising/public relations firm in Chicago, Sid jumped at the opportunity. At that point in time, each office was on their own HR information system which, for a global company, made it very difficult to manage human resources. Sid's first project was to design curriculum, train, and implement a global human resource management software system in 20 international markets and roll out the training program to 10 additional markets after the initial training was completed.

In terms of a global initiative, this was the largest project Sid had ever managed and he knew it will be a challenge. The audience included 25 HR managers speaking 20 different languages. Sid was responsible for all aspects of the training including logistical coordination of training facilities, hospitality (hotels, food, travel), transportation to and from the office, instructional media, training materials, facilitation, enrollments, tracking enrollments, and so on.

The 25 HR managers represent highly diverse backgrounds such as Russian, French, Italian, Japanese, Asian, and Middle Eastern. While the primary language in this company is English, Sid has to consider how to support trainees whose first language was not English. Sid knew all training materials would be written in English and because of Sid's cultural competency, he also knew it was important to develop training materials that were culturally sensitive and at the same time represented real life situations the HR managers encounter, so they could apply what they learned in training when back at their offices.

Sid thought it important to incorporate a change management component in the training and focus on how system changes impact both the people in the organization and their business processes. Additionally, he knew it was important to consider cultural differences in communication style and learning style of the trainees, prepare meaningful training materials, consider food restrictions, figure out trainee work schedules, and make accommodation for the holidays and holy days of the 25 different HR managers attending the initial training.

Sid was excited and thought that for some attending the session, it would be a treat to come to Chicago for a week and be trained. He wondered if he should look at doing some sort of tour of the city and plan after-hours functions for the group. Sid said, "the funny thing about this job is that I don't have staff and it is the first time I am single-handedly pulling together everything myself."

While the company doesn't have a global training and organizational development program, there is discussion about moving Sid out of his current role and helping the firm develop global training in organizational development. While Sid has been in the position for less than a year, this would be a promotion and he is thinking the success of this training program would certainly help his chances at the promotion.

General Question:

1. Consider the training program Sid is about to develop. If you were in Sid's position, what do you perceive as being important in preparing for this training program?

Discussion Questions:

1. In terms of training plan, timelines, travel logistics, facilities, technical support, communication with trainees, etc. how will Sid determine what to work on first?

2. To what extent does the cultural composition and diversity of the participants make a difference in how Sid will prepare for the training program?

3. How might learning and communications styles be considered when Sid begins to lay out and prepare the training curriculum and materials?

4. What (if anything) should Sid to do accommodate the variety of language differences for the trainees during the training program?

5. What challenges might Sid encounter when introducing a change management component into the training?

6. How will Sid set up the training classroom, and what type of instructional media should he use?

7. Why should Sid consider doing hospitality and creature comforts during training?

8. When facilitating the training, what are some of the options Sid should include when presenting the course to the trainees? Personal presentation strategies including movement, eye contact, proximity, effective use of voice, and so on.

9. How important is it to consider how adults from different cultures learn? Why is this important?

10. What types of evaluations should Sid put in place to assess the training?

Case prepared by Marijo Pesch, PhD, of the University of Colorado Hospital in Denver, CO.

Case: Program Planning at Harper Bank

Jean Moore works in training and development in the human resource department at the main headquarters of Harper Bank. Although she aspires to a management position in training, she had only been with the bank for a year, so her main responsibilities include planning and conducting various training programs for bank employees. Because she earned a master's degree in adult learning and development, she is well-respected by her peers and management as an effective facilitator and trainer in staff workshops and as an efficient program planner as well. Through her work, Jean has developed collegial relationships with many of the staff and management, including the president of the bank, Vanessa Jones.

As the bank has grown, some communication problems among staff and management team members have become apparent, particularly during the past few months, and there have been incidents that have escalated to anger between staff members, bank managers, and bank customers. Many of the misunderstandings seem to be driven by employees' not understanding or disregarding the racial, cultural, or ethnic backgrounds of other employees or customers. In addition, because of lack of cultural awareness and sensitivity, some front-line bank employees have been involved in unpleasant situations with customers in the bank, resulting in customers transferring their accounts to other banks.

Bank management, including Vanessa Jones, have become increasingly aware of these problems and have looked to the human resources department and the training staff. The training programs designed to address these issues were developed several years ago by members of the training department other than Jean; these programs deliver content in a non-interactive, lecture-only mode to program participants. Although the programs have been delivered regularly over the past several years, they are viewed by participants as somewhat of a "joke" and thus have not improved employees' understandings of culture, race, or ethnicity nor their skills in working with people of diverse backgrounds. In the current training program, a typical 2-hour long communication training session, the instructional plan consists of the following:

- Introduction of topic by trainer;
- Paper and pencil training pre-test concerning good communication skills;
- PowerPoint presentation of effective communication skills; trainer reads the slides to the attendees;
- Brief question and answer session;

- Posttest of communication skills; and
- Attendees receive a copy of the PowerPoint slides from the trainer as they return to their work stations.

The perceived ineffective training program, coupled with increasing communication issues which have resulted in customer dissatisfaction with the banks, have resulted in increasing frustration among all staff and management members. Vanessa Jones has expressed her displeasure with the ineffective training to the management team. She also feels that Richard Less, the head of the human resource division which houses the training department, has ignored her concerns for the past 6 months by not assigning any members of the training staff to address these issues and redesign the communication/cultural sensitivity training program.

Finally, after the presentation of another communication/cultural sensitivity training course that failed to produce any improvements in communication and understanding among management and staff members, Ms. Jones decides to force a change to this training program. Frustrated with the lack of improvement in this workshop despite her requests for change, she decides to by-pass Mr. Less and capitalize on Jean Moore's knowledge of adult education and program planning. Ms. Jones sends a memo to Ms. More, detailing her concerns about the current, ineffective communication and cultural awareness training workshop. Ms. Jones asks Ms. Moore to develop a "new and improved" workshop, emphasizing that she wants the program planning to proceed and the workshop to be developed and presented within the next 30 days. She asks Ms. Moore to use her extensive knowledge of learning in adulthood and planning programs for adult learners to develop and facilitate this new communication/cultural sensitivity training workshop.

Discussion Questions:

1. How should Jean Moore respond to Vanessa Jones' request to plan the training program?
2. Discuss power and interests that are apparent in both the bank and in the program planning process.
3. Assuming that Jean Moore plans the communication/cultural sensitivity workshop, describe the planning process she might use. In other words, how might she determine the purpose/objectives of the program and learning objectives, and what might the instructional design and delivery strategies look like?

4. How should Jean Moore assess this workshop? What kinds of data would be useful to collect that would help the bank decide if the program is successful? Who should Jean Moore invite to help her plan the program? Why should these people be included?

5. How does this workshop planning demonstrate good program planning? Detail the issues that were addressed and resolved during the planning process? Whose interests are present at the planning table and during the planning process? How are they represented? In what ways can Ms. Moore ensure that all necessary voices are heard during planning?

6. What leadership framework seems to be the operating mode of this bank? Is it appropriate? Why or why not? Describe the different roles that Vanessa Jones, Jean Moore, and Richard Less seem to play in the organization.

Case prepared by Catherine Hansman, EdD, of Cleveland State University in Cleveland, OH.

PROGRAM EVALUATION

Case: Back to the Basics

Case: Dalton City—Program Evaluation

Case: Back to the Basics

Emily is an educational program manager for a large nonprofit organization, with branch offices and centers all over the United States. Last year, the organization secured a large grant used to fund training programs that would be offered to unemployed and displaced workers in four cities around the United States. Those cities were Dallas, Las Vegas, Sacramento, and Detroit. Emily had worked with educational programmers at the organization's offices in those four cities to develop training programs that focused on the teaching of basic workplace skills. General topics covered in these courses included basic computer program usage, spelling and grammar, and math skills. Content on the job-seeking process, including how to complete a job application and how to effectively interview for a job was also included. All programs contained some core content that was the same in every city, along with some specialized content that was determined important in each of the cities in which the courses were held. All ran for four weeks, with instruction 20 hours per week. Classes were held in the late afternoons so attendees could devote their days to their job searches.

The success of the program was to be evaluated by the number of people who completed the course and the number who were successful in obtaining employment following completion of the course.

Emily had recently gathered data for this evaluation, and was reviewing the numbers. Table 3.2 presents the findings:

Table 3.2.

Month	City	Started Program	Completed Program	Found Job
February	Dallas	25	20	12
	Las Vegas	30	21	10
	Sacramento	25	11	7
	Detroit	25	12	5
March	Dallas	25	118	10
	Las Vegas	30	15	7
	Sacramento	25	12	6
	Detroit	25	10	4
April	Dallas	25	15	9
	Las Vegas	30	17	5
	Sacramento	25	15	10
	Detroit	25	8	2

Discussion Questions:

1. What do these statistics tell you about each individual program?
2. At each location, what are some external factors that might affect program completion and the number of completers who actually found jobs?
3. At each location, what are some internal factors that might affect program completion and the number of completers who actually found jobs?
4. What other data might Emily collect to analyze as part of her evaluation process? How would that data be collected?

Case prepared by Steven W. Schmidt, PhD, of East Carolina University in Greenville, NC.

Case: Dalton City—Training Program Evaluation

Items to review: Dalton City Overview
Dalton City Needs Assessment Case Study
Dalton City Training Program Development Case Study

Review all of the items about Dalton City noted above, and consider the following questions:

Discussion Question:

1. How would you propose to evaluate the customer service training program that Carol is developing?
2. How would you evaluate the supervisory training program that Carol is purchasing?

Case prepared by Elizabeth S. Knott, EdD, of East Carolina University in Greenville, NC.

CAREER DEVELOPMENT

Case: The List

Case: It's a Breeze

Case: The Next Move

Case: The List

Sam stared at the list of names that had been e-mailed to him a few minutes earlier. Before taking a new job 3 years ago, he had been a 20-year employee of Titan Corporation, a recreational vehicle manufacturer that was now laying off employees in response to an economic downturn. Recreational vehicles were a luxury item, and for the first time in many years, the organization found itself in a position in which it had to revise its overall business strategy in order to survive. That strategy included consolidating some manufacturing operations, outsourcing its warehousing and distribution facilities, and reducing the size of its employee base, which had numbered approximately 7,000.

The employees at the organization's corporate headquarters had been told several weeks ago that job cuts were on the horizon, and starting earlier in the week, employees whose jobs were being eliminated were called to the human resources department with their supervisors to discuss the ending of their jobs. It had been a difficult week for all employees of the organization, as names of exiting employees and stories about individual termination meetings began to circulate. Several employees began keeping lists of the terminated employees, and it was one of those lists that had been forwarded to Sam. By the time Sam saw the list, it included approximately 40 names, and that wasn't even a complete list.

Sam reflected on his time with Titan as he looked at the names on the list. He had worked in the corporate offices of Titan for many years, and had enjoyed his time there. He had worked there during good economic times, during a period when Titan's products were extremely popular. Often during those times, the company could not keep up with customer demand, and it had made major expansions to its facilities in response to this demand. The company also grew fairly rapidly, although its management was fairly fiscally conservative, so the growth was tempered somewhat by what the market would bear in both the short and longer terms.

During those times company benefits were very generous, and the company was regarded as a desirable place to work. Sam was the hiring manager for many people during his tenure at Titan, and the number of resumes he received in response to job postings had been at times overwhelming. The company had offered full insurance benefits, liberal vacation policies, and many opportunities for advancement. Its career management department worked to help employees who were interested to develop skills for both present and future jobs. In order to prepare its workforce for jobs in the organization, it also offered generous educational benefits, including full tuition reimbursement programs for college courses at many levels. In fact, Sam had taken advantage of the company's tuition reimbursement program to attain an advanced degree while he worked there.

The degree that Sam attained while at Titan helped him to move up in the organization. It also prepared him for opportunities outside of the organization, and when one such opportunity presented itself, Sam took it. He made a major career change, and was now in a different type of organization, doing work he enjoyed. Still, he remained close to several people at Titan, and kept track of what was going on at his old organization. It was because of those contacts that he was able to keep track of what was going on at Titan today.

As Sam reviewed the list of names, he looked for commonalities or themes in the types of employees who had been dismissed from the organization. Most were lower or mid-level employees, although there were a few upper-level employees on the list too. Several of the names on the list had been employees of Sam's when he worked at Titan, and were at best, poor to mediocre performers (in Sam's opinion). They lacked the skills, abilities, and/or motivation to do the job. Their performance was not poor enough for outright termination on those grounds, but they were not very effective either. Some of those employees were simply in the wrong jobs. They had adequate skill sets in general, but for one reason or another, found themselves in jobs for which they were not extremely well qualified. The difficulty that employees in those positions faced was that their reputations in those jobs precluded them from moving anywhere else within the organization. That resulted in them being "stuck" in their positions.

The ones on the list that Sam felt particularly bad for were those employees who had been with the organization for long periods of time. He recognized several names of employees who had been with the organization for 20 to 30 years. Those employees had started with Titan right out of high school, and had been loyal to the company for a long time. Sam knew it would be difficult for them to find comparable jobs now. These employees had built up years of seniority that resulted in salaries and vacation time that probably could not be matched anywhere else at this point. Most of them had been good employees who had either stayed in lower-level or moved to mid-level positions with the organization. They had solid work experience, but at this point, most were in their 40s and 50s, and with only high school educations, they would probably have difficulty finding employment in these depressed economic times.

Still others had been good employees who found themselves in departments that were being downsized or eliminated. Sam had heard that some of these employees were given opportunities in other parts of the company, but some were on the list as well. There were also rumors of future cuts that would be made several months from now; however, those rumors had not been confirmed.

Discussion Questions:

1. What lessons in career development can you learn from this case?
2. What is the role of the organization and of the individual in the career development process?
3. Assume you are a career counselor at Titan Corporation today. How would you advise existing employees about career development during difficult economic times? If you had been a career counselor at Titan Corporation 20 years ago and had been counseling people whose names appeared on the list today, what advice would you have given them?

Case prepared Steven W. Schmidt, PhD, of East Carolina University in Greenville, NC.

Case: It's a Breeze

Matilda just received her master's degree in human resource development (HRD) and was happy to get a small consulting job for an international resort company, Breeze. The North American branch of Breeze consisted of 17 resorts in 12 countries located in North America, South America, and the Caribbean. She met with Mike, director of training of the North American branch, who introduced the problem and explained Matilda's task.

Breeze had a tradition of promoting employees from within: New employees were hired as associates and if merited, were gradually promoted to supervisory positions. In fact, Mike started his career at Breeze as an associate, working as a swimming instructor 25 years earlier. When he got the director of training position, he realized that Breeze did not have a formal system to objectively assess employee skills in order to advance them from one position to another. Mike was working on developing such system.

This new system divided employee career tracks at Breeze into three levels. Level 1 focused on career advancement within a service area (Breeze had several dozen service areas at each resort, including daycare, reception, swimming, kayaking, and gift shops). Level 2 focused on career advancement across service areas within one resort. Level 3 included advancement across different resorts and/or to headquarters.

Since most jobs at Breeze were at Level 1, Mike's priority was to develop tools to assess employee skills at Level 1 for all service areas. Level 1 for every service area consisted of three steps. The career path at Level 1 worked as follows: Each employee started as an associate (Step 1), could be promoted to an assistant manager position (Step 2), and further up to the manager position (Step 3). Employees completed Step 1 when they demonstrated that they could perform all duties of an associate of the service area without direct supervision. Employees completed Step 2 when they demonstrated that they could supervise a small team of Associates of the service area. Employees completed Step 3 when they demonstrated that they could supervise all daily operations of the service area.

To assess employee performance at each step, a tool called "Breeze Competencies" was developed. Breeze Competencies for each step consisted of a checklist that outlined the goal and objectives of the assessment and listed detailed competencies that were grouped in several categories and subcategories. For example, some of the categories in Step 1 of the service area called Daycare included communication, safety and security, and facilities. The communication category was divided into communication with other associates, communication with assistant manager and manager, and communication with customers. Each competency was graded on the scale of 1 to 3. Decisions on employees' potential for advancement (from any level to the next) were based on a total score.

Matilda's task was to develop Level 1 Breeze Competencies checklists for the service area called Bar—one checklist for each of the three steps (i.e., associate, assistant manager, and manager). At each resort, the bar service area was opened from 9 A.M. until late at night and was a part of the dining facility. Customers had free breakfast, lunch, and dinner at the dining facility and could purchase alcoholic and nonalcoholic drinks at the bar.

At the end of the meeting, Mike gave Matilda the following materials that could help her with the task:

- Breeze competencies checklists for two service areas, Daycare and Reception, to use as examples;
- A job orientation manual that all employees at all service areas received on their first day on the job; and
- A Bar Associate's Training Manual that all new bar employees received on their first day on the job. This manual explained the basic duties of the bar associate's job.

Mike explained that it was a busy season at Breeze but he set up a date for Matilda to drive to one of the closest Breeze resorts and talk to several employees. The schedule of Matilda's resort visit was the following:

- Fifteen-20 minutes with the bar manager, who would show her some of the resort facilities and the bar;
- Thirty minutes to observe the work of the bar associates;
- One-hour focus group interview with the bar manager and two bar associates; and
- Thirty-minute lunch with the assistant bar manager and the same two bar associates.

Matilda had 1 week to study the materials that Mike gave her and 3 more weeks after her resort visit to develop drafts of the three competencies checklists.

General Question:

1. Matilda have never had a vacation at *Breeze* and never worked at a bar or a restaurant. If you were Matilda, how would you use the materials and the resort visit to create the three competencies checklists?

Discussion Questions:

1. How should Matilda use the Breeze materials that Mike gave her? What kind of information would you expect to find in each of these materials?
2. What questions should she ask the focus group? What questions should she ask each of the members of the group individually (bar manager, bar associates, and assistant bar manager)?
3. What should she look for when she observes the work of the bar associates?
4. What would be included on your list of competencies for each of the three levels? What types of competencies would you add for each increasing level? How can continuity or progression of competencies (and categories) from one level to the next be ensured?
5. What difficulties might Matilda encounter while working on the task?

Case prepared by Maria (Masha) S. Plahotnik of Florida International University in Miami, FL.

Case: The Next Move

Joe Simon's Career Aspirations at CPL

Joe Simon was due for his 4-year performance review at CPL Ltd., a small-scale domestic producer and marketer of consumer products in the United States. CPL's product line includes detergents, soap, shampoos, and cosmetic products and its workforce consists of leadership, managerial employees and unionized labor. Joe joined CPL as a management trainee in human resources (HR) after completing his MBA in human resource management and was made an assistant manager of human resources in his second year in the organization. Joe enjoys working as an HR practitioner at CPL and had gained expertise in almost all HR functions including recruitment, training, employee development, and labor relations, during his 4 years in the department. His performance in managing labor relations had been especially noteworthy. The relationship between the labor union and management at CPL was quite tumultuous before Joe came on board. Joe took an impressive initiative in improving labor relations by involving the factory staff in planning opportunities for their training and development at CPL. His efforts made the factory employees feel valued and empowered.

As a next step in his career at CPL, Joe aspired to make HR a strategic function by gaining a holistic understanding of CPL's business operations. He knew that a lateral promotion to a position in the operations department would provide him with such knowledge. He was contemplating that his 4-year performance review might offer him an opportunity of requesting such a lateral promotion. He felt that working in operations would help him build stronger relationships with the factory staff, understand the dynamics in the supply chain management at CPL, and plan for how HR can be better aligned with the business strategy at CPL.

CPL's Career Development Practice

CPL is known for its progressive performance management practices that align employees' career development with the strategic needs of the business. For instance, they have a "Panel Review" process as a part of the performance management system that is tied to the career development of employees at CPL. In the panel review, senior management reviews the career aspirations of high performers for consideration for assignments both in and outside of their current functions. Employees' career aspirations, as noted in their performance appraisals, are taken into consideration before senior management engages in the panel review process for deciding any upward or lateral career development steps for an employee. The outcome of this review process is a long term career development path for each employee who has a consistent performance record. The career path can be either upward or lateral and depends on both the employee's developmental needs and CPL's requirements.

Organizational Culture and the Strategic Role of HR

Joe arrived early to his cubicle on the day of his performance review. He had prepared a formal letter explaining how the opportunity for a lateral promotion in the Operations department would help to make the HR department a strategic business partner at CPL. He intended to share the letter with his supervisor during his performance feedback meeting. Joe's supervisor, Thomas Smith, was also his informal mentor and took pride in Joe's achievements and good performance at CPL. Joe had informally discussed the prospect of a lateral promotion with Thomas a couple of times before. Thomas's support in this matter had given him confidence about a potential opportunity in the Operations Department.

Thomas seemed a little pensive when Joe walked into his office on Tuesday morning for the performance feedback meeting. He was leaning his forehead on his palms and staring out at the gloomy sky. The downpour outside had abated into a light drizzle now, but the murky weather reminded Thomas about how helpless he had felt during the panel review meeting the day before. He had never foreseen such strong opposition from his peers and superiors against Joe's lateral promotion proposal. Apparently, Thomas's peers in the operations department and his superiors did not feel any need for Joe to join the staff in operations in the near or distant future. They were content with Joe's progress in the HR department and were favoring Joe's upward progression within the department. They were apprehensive that transferring Joe to operations might harm the credibility of the HR department among the factory staff, who shared certain camaraderie with Joe. Thomas clearly remembered how concerned and displeased the vice president, Samuel Petrosko, had sounded in the meeting. "Brace yourself " he had said, "It is mainly due to Joe that the factory staff have started to trust the HR department. Moving Joe out of the department might again make the unions hostile toward HR policies. Moreover, they might perceive Joe's transfer into operations as intrusive and might misunderstand HR's intentions as interfering with their day-to-day tasks. I really don't see why you want to rock the ship when everything is running smoothly. Besides, why does HR need to know the supply chain management tasks carried out by the operations department anyway?"

Although Thomas had counterargued that the factory staff would not perceive Joe's lateral promotion as intrusive because they trusted Joe, he had sensed that the issue was much more serious. It was a cultural issue that went beyond the apprehension of disturbing labor relations. He knew that although there had been lateral promotions at CPL before, there had been very few movements between HR and other support departments in the organization, except at an administrative level. This reflected the fact that, unlike other functional departments at CPL, HR was becoming an increasingly specialist discipline. For the same reasons, staff didn't typically move into HR from other functions of CPL as well. This perception of viewing HR as a specialist function went against Joe's efforts to make HR a strategic department at CPL. Thomas knew that such lack of lateral movement between HR and other departments would lead to a disconnect between HR and other departments at CPL and ultimately a disconnect between HR and the business strategy of CPL.

Thomas shared the outcomes of the panel review meeting with Joe. He explained that the senior management was very impressed with Joe's performance and had recommended him for a lucrative promotion within the HR department. However, the proposal for training Joe for a lateral promotion to a position in the operations department was rejected by majority in the review meeting.

Discussion Questions:

1. What specific factors was Thomas referring to when he noted that the issue at CPL was cultural? What are the cultural barriers against promoting lateral movements between HR and other departments at CPL?

2. If you were Thomas, what steps would you take to increase lateral movements between HR and other departments of CPL in future?

3. How would you convince the VP about the need for Joe to learn about other functions (e.g., operations) at CPL in order to make HR at CPL more strategic?

4. What are the differences between a specialist and a strategic function? If you were Joe, how would you contemplate changing HR's image from a specialist to a strategic function at CPL? What steps would you take?

5. What functions of HR (e.g., recruitment, training, employee development, performance management) do you believe can be better aligned with CPL's business strategy if there are more lateral move-

ments between HR and other functional departments at CPL? Explain.

Case prepared by Rajashi Ghosh, PhD, of Drexel University in Philadelphia, PA.

ORGANIZATIONAL DEVELOPMENT

Case: Out of the Blue

Case: All is not Sunny

Case: The Quality Plan

Case: Out of the Blue

Gabriela is an organizational development consultant. She works with companies, nonprofit organizations, government entities, and educational institutions to assist them in improving their organizations. Gabriela prefers to work collaboratively with her clients, working together to develop solutions, rather than telling them exactly what to do. She feels that this approach results in better solutions to the clients' problems.

Gabriela is consulting with the technical sales department of a medium-sized manufacturing organization, Blue Lake Industrial Products. Blue Lake makes a variety of advanced technical products used in factories. The technical sales team at Blue Lake is responsible for selling the entire range of technical products manufactured by the company.

Recently, Carla, the technical sales director at Blue Lake, has become concerned that the technical sales staff has been struggling to stay informed with the rapid development of new technologies. Carla believes that the training and development process used in the department is no longer adequate to keep up with the rapid pace of change in their customers' industries, and in Blue Lake's product lines. Consequently, Carla contracted with Gabriela to assist her in redeveloping the training and development process for her department. Gabriela has expertise in training and development program planning and is excited about the project.

After a few meetings between Gabriela and Carla, both agreed that an important first step would be to better understand the shortcomings in the current training and development process for the technical sales staff. Gabriela and Carla worked together collaboratively in several conversations and developed a long list of questions that they wanted to ask the technical sales staff. Some of the key questions were as follows. How well do you feel you are able to keep up with Blue Lake's new product roll-outs? How well prepared are you to talk about changes in your customers' industries and operations that affect their needs for our products? In what areas do you feel you need additional training? The answers to these questions would be used to decide what should be done to improve the training and development process for the technical sales staff.

Carla felt strongly that an online survey to the technical sales people would be the best way to gather the answers to these questions. Gabriela, on the other hand, based on her expertise in this area, felt that an online survey would be inefficient and cumbersome for the kinds of questions being asked. Gabriela felt strongly that talking to the sales staff individually and in groups would provide the information needed most effectively and efficiently. When Gabriela gently raised the possibility of these in-person meetings, Carla wasn't interested. Instead Carla indicated that she thought that an online survey would be better.

Gabriela feels that she has a dilemma. On the one hand, she feels strongly that an online survey would not be useful to get the kind of information that is needed for Carla and Blue Lake to improve their training process for the technical sales staff. On the other hand, she respects Carla's opinion and wants to work collaboratively rather than telling Carla what to do.

Gabriela feels that she has several options:

- Gabriela can tell Carla that she really feels strongly that she should get this information through in-person individual and group meetings. Gabriela can say that although she respects Carla's point of view, Gabriela's advice is that in-person individual and group meetings would be best in this situation.

- Gabriela can explain more clearly why she disagrees with Carla's suggestion of an online survey and provide some examples to support her view. Gabriela can try to convince Carla to change her mind to Gabriela's view.

- Even though Gabriela thinks that it would not be an efficient approach, Gabriela can go with Carla's view and agree to use an online survey.

General Question:

1. If you were Gabriela, how would you approach this dilemma? Would you use one of the options listed above or do you have another approach that Gabriela has not considered?

Discussion Questions:

1. What should be Gabriela's goals and most important priorities when she is deciding which of the above options to choose?

2. What are the advantages and disadvantages of the options listed above, as well as any additional options that you think would be helpful for Gabriela?

3. What do you think might happen in the short-term and the long-term with her relationship with Carla and with the success of the consulting project if Gabriela took each of these options?

4. What would be your course of action if you were Gabriela?

Case prepared by Brian Altman and Simone Conceicao, PhD, both of the University of Wisconsin–Milwaukee in Milwaukee, WI.

Case: All is not Sunny

The Problem

The Sunnydew County Public School System recognized that it has a principal problem. Specifically, its K-12 principals were retiring or leaving the profession in alarming rates. Moreover, the role of the principal has transformed because of economic, demographic, technological, and global pressures. These changes, in addition to the focus on accountability for student achievement, have exposed skill deficits in Sunnydew's principals. In response, some principals are choosing to leave the profession and others are choosing to retire. The Sunnydew Public School system will soon face a principal shortage and is engaging in efforts to mitigate this problem.

The Organizational Development Intervention

Among the many efforts aimed at fixing the principal problem is a long-term effort to develop a competency model that specifies principal performance requirements. In other words, this competency model would specify in behavioral terms, what a Sunnydew K-12 principal should know and be able to do in the execution of their roles and responsibilities. Further, the competency model would serve as a basis for the recruitment, selection, and advancement of principals within the Sunnydew Public school system. Using the organizational development concept of networked organizations, the Sunnydew Public School System partnered with a large state-funded university to develop the competency model. A design team was formed consisting of senior officials of the Sunnydew Public School System and the university. Specifically, members of the design team included principals, district administrators, university administrators, and professors who taught in the educational administration program at the university. The design team was chartered and as part of this charter was required to report its outputs to the superintendant of Sunnydew County Public Schools and the dean of the university's college of education. The mission of the design team's charter was to develop a human resource-based competency model that specifies the performance requirements for aspiring, beginning and experienced principals.

Status Quo

The design team worked consistently for approximately eighteen months to produce a human resource-based competency model. As the team progressed in its work, it used a plan, do, check, and act (PDCA) cycle to ensure that its work outputs were satisfactory to school system and university stakeholders. In addition, the superintendant and the school of education's dean were kept up to date with regular briefing reports. The competency model was developed but was never used within the Sunnydew County Public School System. The Sunnydew County Public School System Superintendant left the school system and the effort was not sustained within the school system. Similarly, the dean at the school of Education left the university and the effort was not sustained at the university as well. The Sunnydew County Public School System still faces a looming principal shortage and the competency model it developed sits on a shelf in a binder somewhere within district offices.

General Question:

1. What factors caused this organizational development intervention to fail?

Discussion Questions:

1. If you were in charge of this initiative, what steps would you have taken to ensure that the organizational development intervention was implemented and sustained?
2. Identify the stakeholders of this organizational development intervention.
3. What role (if any) might community-based organizations play in sustaining this organizational development intervention?
4. How would you feel if you were a member of the design team?

Case prepared by Ray K. Haynes, PhD, of Indiana University in Bloomington, IN.

Case: The Quality Plan

Becoming a Six Sigma Organization

Innovation Appliances is one of the largest global manufacturers of major appliances for the home. Their product lines include refrigerators, cooking appliances, dishwashers, and laundry equipment such as washers and dryers. The home appliances industry is highly competitive and globalized. It is now facing consolidation and declining profit margins for a majority of its product lines. In view of this operating environment, Ian Forward, the chief executive officer of Innovation Appliances, has decided to transform Innovation Appliances in to a Six Sigma organization. Six Sigma is a business management strategy aimed at reducing variance or defects in process outputs (Pande & Holpe, 2002). Since Innovation Appliances relies heavily on manufacturing process to produce its products, Ian Forward believes that Six Sigma's quality management methods when applied to Innovation Appliances manufacturing processes would reduce defects, increase quality outputs, and serve as a competitive advantage for the foreseeable future.

In efforts to diffuse Six Sigma throughout Innovation Appliances, Mr. Forward has created a new executive position (vice president of Six Sigma & Quality) and has hired Tanya Able to lead the diffusion and implementation of Six Sigma throughout Innovation Appliances. Ms. Able, an experienced electrical engineer and Six Sigma Master Black understands that the implementation and successful adoption of Six Sigma requires that the adopting organization create an infrastructure of people to train and develop employees of the organization in the Six Sigma methodology. Ms. Able, an earnest, abrasive, and no-nonsense executive, proceeds with her charge to diffuse and transform Innovation Appliances into a Six Sigma manufacturing organization. She employed a strategy for creating a Six Sigma people infrastructure by selecting the seemingly best and the brightest from the ranks of upper and midlevel management. These individuals then received training to become Master Black Belts, Black Belts and Green Belts. In the lexicon of Six Sigma, individuals with the title of Master Black belt are responsible for training Black Belts, Green Belts, and others in the Six Sigma methodology. Black Belts and Green Belts are responsible for executing Six Sigma Projects aimed at reducing variance and improving quality in a manufacturing process.

The Innovation Appliances Culture

Innovation Appliances workforce consists of leadership, managerial employees and represented (unionized) labor. As is typical of the home appliances industry, the Innovation Appliances labor force has seen decade by decade declines since the 1970s. Moreover, labor relations between management and the union have been tense, hostile and guarded as profit margins shrink; the labor force declines and product lines are relocated to overseas manufacturing facilities. Human Resources within Innovation Appliances can now be characterized as factions made up of leadership, management, and unionized labor.

Ms. Able's Six Sigma Infrastructure

Ms. Able has been successful in creating her Six Sigma infrastructure. She has hired individuals from all of Innovation Appliances divisions and departments to serve as Master Black Belts, Black Belts, and Green Belts. Furthermore, she has developed a communication strategy promoting these individuals as high-potential employees of the organization. The promotion of these individuals has continued for several months and the training in the Six Sigma methodology is well underway.

One afternoon, after a lunch meeting with Tom Changeman, Innovation Appliances' Vice President of Learning and Performance, Ms. Able learns that the labor force is not happy with the transformation to Six Sigma. Mr. Forward tells Ms. Able that a good majority of the labor force thinks that the individuals she has selected for her Six Sigma infrastructure have been selected for purposes of eliminating their jobs. Moreover the labor force does not see Six Sigma as a quality improvement tool. Rather, they see it as a job elimination scheme. Ms. Able appeared genuinely shocked by this information and began to ponder her next steps in moving toward transforming Innovation Appliances into a Six Sigma Organization.

General Question:

1. In considering Ms. Able's actions for creating the Six Sigma infrastructure, what did she do wrong and what corrective actions would you suggest she take? What did she do well?

Discussion Questions:

1. Is this an organizational development issue? Why or why not?
2. Which group of Innovation Appliances stakeholders would be most affected by the diffusion and adoption of Six Sigma?

3. What level of change (e.g., individual, group, organization) would you say is occurring at Innovation appliances?

4. If you were in Ms. Able's shoes, what types of help would you solicit and from whom?

REFERENCE

Pande, P., & Holpp, L., (2002). *What is Six Sigma?* New York, NY: McGraw Hill.

Case prepared by Ray K. Haynes, PhD, of Indiana University in Bloomington, IN, and Rajashi Ghosh, PhD, of Drexel University in Philadelphia, PA.

WORKPLACE DIVERSITY AND CULTURAL COMPETENCE

Case: Laying the Groundwork

Case: The Night Out

Case: The Divided Campus

Case: The Guest Speaker

Case: The Performance Review

Case: Laying the Groundwork

Derek Jordan was in his third year as a human resources specialist at Central Associated Manufacturing (CAM), a large supplier of components for heavy equipment manufacturers. Derek was located at CAM-Deering, one of the largest manufacturing facilities in the company, which opened 80 years ago and currently has 900 employees. The facility is located in Deering, a small midwestern city, and draws most of its employees from the surrounding rural communities. Among the current employee base, the average length of service is 14 years. Although the company has very high expectations for employees, individuals have historically been loyal to the company due to excellent pay and benefits and because of strong feelings of camaraderie among employees.

CAM-Deering was formerly an independent family-owned company, but was acquired by CAM about 20 years ago. The Deering facility has a long, proud history and consistently outperforms competitors and other divisions in the company. In fact, the division was allowed to operate as an independent subsidiary for over 10 years, with little changing from when it was an independent company. Ten years ago, the entire company began a major restructuring. The presidents of each subsidiary were removed and most functions within the company were centralized. As a result of this centralization, CAM-Deering lost the accounting, marketing, product development, and information technology departments, among other support functions. This has resulted in nearly 800 positions in Deering being gradually eliminated in 10 years. The remaining departments at Deering are the various manufacturing departments, human resources, building and equipment maintenance, safety, and the office of the general manager (formerly director of manufacturing).

After most of the restructuring was complete, CAM-Deering was productive and most remaining employees were still very loyal to the company. However, the upper management saw weaknesses in the facility. First, a "good ol' boys network" seemed to permeate the facility. This system caused some problems to be overlooked due to personal familiarity and favoritism. Second, due to long personal histories and alliances, employees oftentimes received promotions based upon personal connections rather than merit. Most significantly, the division had longstanding problems with racist, sexist, and homophobic incidents. Although the company did begin to diversify its employee ranks after an employment discrimination lawsuit in the 1970s, significant problems persisted and these incidents were not taken as seriously as they should have been taken. As a result of these problems, a new general manager was hired 6 years ago, with a charge to fix these problems and lead CAM-Deering into a new era.

The new general manager steadily replaced many of the problematic managers and built a new management team. Significant changes occurred throughout the facility. Expectations were equalized among employees, management favoritism decreased, efficiencies were introduced, and production expectations rose. These changes brought resentment from many of those who were formerly favored. Additionally, nearly all employees disliked the increased production expectations. Employees grew weary of the ongoing rounds of downsizing in the front office complex, as the division's employee count was cut in half. However, most employees recognized that their jobs were more secure since they worked in the core function of this highly profitable manufacturing facility.

Derek was part of the new wave of management employees at CAM-Deering. The HR department built a reputation among hourly employees and management as a well-run department where good service was emphasized. The HR staff was strongly committed to the importance of having a diverse workforce and emphasized recruitment, education, and policies that would help to foster a diverse culture.

Although great progress was made regarding diversity issues, lingering problems persisted. For example, a noose was hung above a workstation of an African American employee. Racist and homophobic graffiti regularly appeared in bathroom stalls. Women were almost completely absent from the highest-paying manufacturing jobs in the facility. The physical demands of the jobs made retaining women difficult. However, women in those positions also faced ridicule from some male employees, resulting in turnover. As a result of these persistent problems, a zero tolerance policy was implemented regarding harassment. Employees engaging in severe forms of harassment were terminated from employment. Although the policy assisted in building a culture that would not tolerate overt harassment, the general manager and the HR group decided that additional steps were needed to help create a culture than truly appreciated diversity.

Derek was assigned the role of developing a plan to increase appreciation for diversity at CAM-Deering. Since the compliance issues had largely been addressed, Derek realized that he was faced with an ambiguous problem that was difficult to pinpoint. He decided to begin this process by conducting a needs assessment to understand the diversity issues facing the division.

Discussion Questions:

1. If you were Derek, how would you conduct a needs assessment to understand this issue?

(a) Who would you involve?
(b) What information/data would you collect?
(c) Who would be the key stakeholders in the needs assessment process?
(d) How would you use the results?
(e) In designing this needs assessment, how would you increase the likelihood of the findings being used?

2. Given the massive restructuring at CAM-Deering, what do you think of the timing of the efforts to create a culture appreciating diversity (since employees might be defensive to any additional forms of change)?

3. How is the diversity issue connected with the broader issue of dismantling the "good ol' boys network?"

4. Through the needs assessment, how could Derek understand the following aspects related to diversity?

(a) Recruitment
(b) Policies
(c) Training/Education
(d) Employee Involvement
(e) Performance Management
(f) Organizational Culture

5. What are the advantages of moving from a compliance approach to diversity to a more proactive approach? What are the challenges with such an approach?

6. How (if at all) does Derek's role differ if he is a member of an underrepresented group (e.g., African American, gay)?

Case prepared by Rod P. Githens, PhD, of the University of Louisville in Louisville, KY, and Rajashi Ghosh, PhD, of Drexel University in Philadelphia, PA.

Case: The Night Out

Sylvia is a 35-year-old White woman who was born and raised in Ohio. She is the director of training and development at a large international investment company in Chicago and is responsible for building the training curriculum for the organization. She works with a culturally diverse population of people, some of whom are of Indian and Pakistani descent and others who represent the Pacific Rim. She has been with the firm eight years and is very experienced in training diverse groups of employees.

Sylvia earned a bachelor's of arts and communication degree from a large midwestern university and has earned a master's degree in communication, focusing on organizational development. Early on in her career, Sylvia spent several years working in the automobile industry in customer service and sales training. While in the automobile industry, she set up training centers for the service-related positions and was influential in bringing to fruition technical training programs for sales representatives. She left the automobile industry and joined an international accounting firm doing change consulting. In this capacity, Sylvia was heavily involved in the design and delivery of training programs that focused on corporate initiatives.

In her current position as the director of training and development, Sylvia said she "travels internationally and is one of the few single people at the company who is willing to travel, willing to explore the world a little bit, willing to know colleagues in other countries." In her current role, she facilitates training sessions dealing with change management and leadership. She admits her favorite program to facilitate deals with communication patterns across cultures. She believes this is an ideal training program because it is set up for a multicultural audience and there is ample opportunity for sharing and understanding communication patterns across cultures. When Sylvia described how she prepares for a training program, she was explicit in her description. She visits the U.S. Government Office of Protocol website to learn about the accepted customs and taboos, body language, religions, and socioeconomic trends of the cultures with whom she will be working. She also tries to get to the country the day before the training so she can get a copy of the local newspaper (if it is printed in English), take a look at the tabloid-type publications to see what is going on in pop culture, and get to a grocery store to see what is on the shelves.

Prior to each session, she gets to know those attending the training by talking with them, learning about their professional backgrounds and what their current jobs entail. She also does a needs assessment to determine gaps in what knowledge, skills, and attitudes trainees currently have with regard to change management and leadership. She uses that information to determine what they need to learn and where they need to when they complete her course.

When Sylvia is training, she can quickly identify the tactile learners, the visual learners, and the auditory learners. She is also skilled at understanding the basic traits of the audience. These characteristics are important, as Sylvia believes in presenting course materials in ways that best meet the needs of the audience. With regard to her teaching style, Sylvia said:

> I don't get too tied to the instructor guide, I don't get really tied to what needs to be covered in a day, because if my participants aren't following me down a certain path, it's not going to be successful for me to force them that way … I am more flexible…. We recently went through a 5-day orientation with two very distinct groups of people; one in July, and one in August. The training design was the same … the conduct on each day was very different. In one instance in the August session, they weren't following me at all; they didn't want to have anything to do with certain types of topics…. I'm not willing to push them through topics that they are not receptive to. I figure, whatever, we'll switch to something else. I'm just very flexible. I've had a ton of hours in the classroom, tons of different experiences, I can pull some of this stuff out of my tool box very quickly…. You have the standardized icebreakers you rely on, the standard things you are just going to try…. You have to be able to mix it up, have fun, be friendly and approachable.

Sylvia considers herself to have a global perspective and to be culturally literate and well versed in cultural norms, values, and beliefs of diverse groups. However, she thought it was important to talk about an experience she had when working with a group in Belgium where she was not so "culturally savvy" in a social event outside of the classroom. Here is what she described:

> My colleague and I had instructed in the Brussels office of our company other times, but the night before we were supposed to do the training session with this team of people, we met them for dinner. We were doing one day of instruction with the group the next day, so I was glad to have the dinner meeting the evening before. I don't know how it happened but there was quite a lot of wine and things started loosening up and we were laughing and joking. There were these guys with different cultural backgrounds from the Netherlands … most of these guys were married but if you are Catholic and married in one part of the country you wear your band on the right hand, if you are Protestant and married you wear the band on the left or something like that … so we couldn't tell who was married and who wasn't…. At one point these guys were getting very, very aggressive about our personal lives and our backgrounds and wanted to know what we were doing later on in the evening and all that kind of stuff. It got to the point

where we were extremely uncomfortable and I kept looking at my colleague and thinking at what point in time do we, without being rude, excuse ourselves from this environment, knowing that we have to maintain credibility in the classroom the next day and get the hell out of here.... But they wouldn't let us leave, they wanted us to continue to go out with them. They suggested moving the party from dinner to the bar ... it was very awkward, because we had been drinking with them ... we used moving to the bar as our opportunity to politely excuse ourselves, but I remember walking out of the restaurant area with my colleague and I couldn't figure out at what point we had lost control to the point where we apparently gave some sort of indication that it was OK to act like this.

The next day we went into the classroom in kind of a worn down position ... the day before we were all prepared to go ... and now it was awkward and I felt bad about the behavior and inappropriate conversation from the night before. I was trying to figure out what the cultural elements were because Belgium, Holland you know, the Upper Netherlands area is really open socially with their values ... but then there is a distinction between how they acted at dinner and how they act in a work environment.... They are very stoic in the business environment. I knew these things and the cultural norms and morés ... I think it was just being respectful, doing what I needed to do, but I felt like we had crossed a boundary, and that I should have known how to act because of my experiences working with culturally diverse groups ... I think that's how I reconciled it in the end ... from then on I just instituted a policy ... if they even say we are go to dinner I'm going to have just minimal alcohol and do the polite thing.

General Question:

1. If you were in Sylvia's position, how would you have reconciled this situation in this case?

Discussion Questions:

1. What are some of the potential consequences of the "night out" on the outcomes of the training?
2. What hurdles will Sylvia and her colleague have to overcome when returning to do additional training in Belgium with the same group of trainees?
3. While Sylvia not only acknowledges the importance of understanding that people are different on many levels, and the cultural diversity of trainees is something she has adapts to very quickly when doing training, she put herself in an awkward situation and

jeopardized her credibility. How might Sylvia avoid an embarrassing situation of this nature in the future?

4. What is the importance of a global perspective when working with diverse cultures on a global level?

5. Is it appropriate that Sylvia (who considers herself to be culturally savvy and to have a global perspective) make the distinction between how the trainees acted at dinner and how they acted in a work environment (and thereby viewing her participation in the dinner conversation as "being respectful and doing what I needed to do" with the trainees)?

6. Should Sylvia change how she approaches learning about and preparing for culturally diverse groups she is going to be training? If so, how?

7. What else can Sylvia do to learn about her trainees to optimize the learning environment for everyone in the future?

Case prepared by Marijo Pesch, PhD, of the University of Colorado Hospital in Denver, CO.

Case: The Divided Campus

State College University (SCU) is an urban institution in a city situated in the mid-south. It has two distinct campuses. The East Campus houses the College of Liberal Arts and Sciences while the West Campus is home to the professional schools of dentistry, nursing, and medicine. While a commuter bus connects the two campuses, there is approximately one mile of city land that divides the two education centers. Within this space are a series of public housing buildings.

Jack Cinders has recently been hired as a staff member for SCU and is undergoing his new staff orientation. Two human resource representatives for SCU are facilitating the orientation meeting. Their presentation turns to an explanation about the geographically divided campus and how the shuttle service works so employees and students can be transported between the two campuses. One of the human resource specialists, Giselle, says to the new employees, "When traveling between the two campuses, you should be aware of your surroundings. I encourage you to take the public transportation option rather than walk because there is a lot of crime in this vicinity. Women, in particular, should not walk. There is a higher crime rate in this area than other parts of the city so please be careful. I don't mean to frighten you but rather to caution you."

Upon hearing his colleague make these remarks, Kevin, the other human resource representative, responds: "I am troubled by your remarks, Giselle. I don't want our new employees to get the wrong idea. Because our campus is separated and the area between West Campus and East Campus has a higher number of residents who are African Americans, Latinos, and Latinas, I think your warning is a bit racist."

Giselle is taken off guard at Kevin's intervention and is left speechless.

General Questions:

1. Is Giselle's original comment a racist one?

Discussion Questions:

1. What does this situation say about race? About gender? About socioeconomic status?

2. As educators, what possible statements might we make that might be considered racist by others? Is a statement racist if the intent was not there? Should we apologize for other people's perceptions?

3. What can we learn from this scenario about constructing our professional knowledge and about our own personal identities?

4. What can we consider about our own professional identities from this incident, understanding that embodiment might play a role in this story as did positionality between authority figures (facilitators) and the "other" (new employees)?

5. Do you think Jack should listen quietly to the exchange or share his opinion about the unfolding situation?

6. How could Giselle have paraphrased her remarks differently, or was a paraphrase even necessary?

7. Do you think Kevin should have intervened as he did, or spoken with Giselle privately?

8. Should a trainer follow a set script of remarks and not deviate from them to avoid unintentional political, emotional, controversial, and volatile statements?

Case prepared by Patrick Finnessy, Ph.D., of the University of Toronto in Toronto, ON.

Case: The Guest Speaker

Elizabeth Hope has been working at ABC Financial Trust for the past year. It is a large banking entity that provides a full range of financial products and services to personal and small business customers. While there are over 1,000 branches across the country, their corporate offices are housed in urban centers; Elizabeth was hired a year ago as a corporate trainer for an east-coast operation with nearly 1,500 employees.

As it is January, the corporate office's training and development center is hosting an event to recognize the upcoming Martin Luther King, Jr. holiday. Elizabeth, who seldom seems to be able to break away from her desk, makes a reservation to attend the luncheon so she can hear the guest speaker and consider her own approaches to workplace diversity. A flier provided to staff members has indicated that a keynote speech titled "Individual Responsibility and Diversity" will be delivered.

Elizabeth attends the event and following the buffet lunch, a fellow staff member introduces the guest speaker. He is welcomed as Reverend Jerome Smith, and his list of pastoral work and civil rights activism is featured in his introduction. When the keynote speaker takes the podium, he begins his remarks by highlighting the work of Reverend King. He speaks about individual responsibility and being accountable for individual actions toward fellow colleagues. He provides an overview of Martin Luther King's work and what we can learn from him. Then, his remarks take a sudden turn.

Rev. Smith's commentary starts to refer to the "Black Cause." He states that the plight of Black workers has been seized by the gay and lesbian community and disrupted the African American movement. He claims that God did not create Adam and Steve but rather Adam and Eve. He punctuates that the workforce must consider the disadvantages affecting the Black man who still does not earn equal pay to the White man, even when the Black man has a family to feed. He argues that recent discussions of same-sex marriage and domestic partnership benefits have usurped honest discussions about racism in the corporate and work environments. He states that gay activists have attempted to piggyback on the civil rights struggles of people of color, even as most of them have not studied those struggles and the legacy of the Civil Rights Movement. He insists that he has heard individuals in the workforce make statements that diminish the impact of racism by always connecting homophobia with racism as if they were the same. He believes that gays want to support racial diversity only when Black folks include sexual identity in their definition of diversity. He closes by arguing that Title VII of the Civil Rights Act of 1964 prohibits employment discrimination on the basis of race and religion and not on sexual orientation, and so the workplace environment must be more vocal about racial inequities and respect religious values rather than promote a gay-friendly agenda.

During the question and answer period following the Reverend's address, Elizabeth raises her hand.

General Question:

1. If you were in Elizabeth's position, would you ask a question or make a statement and what would your chosen words be?

Discussion Questions:

1. Does Reverend Smith have a point? What points might he have? Do you think he errs in any judgment?
2. What *is* the definition of diversity?
3. What *is* our individual responsibility in addressing issues of diversity in the workplace?
4. Is there a hierarchy of identity markers when addressing issues connected to diversity? Should there be? Why or why not?
5. What is the responsibility of the individual who has invited Reverend Smith to speak? What should this person's follow-up be?
6. What comments would you make on a written evaluation about the day's event?
7. How should this event be followed-up or is any follow-up necessary?
8. How does one's personal identity inform and construct one's professional identity?
9. Is it important to understand how a people's history inspires one's view on issues of sexuality, sexual identity, gender identity, and religion/spirituality? Do these discussions have a place in the workplace setting? Why or why not?
10. Do you think racism and heterosexism is the same thing (or similar)? Do White lesbian, gay, bisexual, and transgender people experience the same type of discrimination as people of color or is the question itself not merited?
11. How might this presentation be connected to policy issues?
12. Should corporate environments protect individuals based on the basis of sexual orientation? Why or why not? Should there be federal protection based on sexual orientation?

13. Are national laws and company policies on race enforced and followed?

14. What, if any, is the intersection between racial and sexual identity?

Case prepared by Patrick Finnessy, PhD, of the University of Toronto in Toronto, ON.

Case: The Performance Review

Sandy has been working as a unionized employee for a manufacturing company on the East Coast for the past 8 years. Sandy is a biological male who self-identifies as an M to F. This means Sandy identifies not as male ("M") but as a female ("F"). Sandy is involved as an activist with a local transgender organization and has been "out" (open about being transgender) at work since hired.

Sandy's legislature has introduced a statewide measure to protect employees based on sexual orientation and gender identity, but it has not yet passed or been enacted. Sandy's employer also has been discussing its own policies on these statuses with no conclusive results.

Sandy's supervisor is Sergio Ramirez, and he is preparing Sandy's annual evaluation review. As he does so, he is reflecting on Sandy's time-on-task regarding job performance. Sergio finds Sandy's contributions in the workplace effective, but he is concerned that, as an administrative assistant, Sandy is absent from the office too frequently.

One of Sergio's primary concerns is the amount of time Sandy takes on breaks. Sandy does not consistently take scheduled breaks (10:00-10:15; 2:30-2:45) as the union allows but instead uses the washroom several times a day as needed. Sergio has learned that Sandy departs from the second-floor office to utilize the washroom on the sixth floor each time. Sandy has explained to Sergio that this is done for safety reasons. Because Sandy is transgender, and members of the trans community experience a higher incidence of violence (especially from male perpetrators), Sandy uses the top-floor women's washroom because they are more removed, more private, and due to the lower traffic flow are perceived by Sandy to be more safe. Each time Sandy leaves the office, this means that Sandy waits for the elevator, rides it, uses the washroom, possibly waits for a stall, waits for the elevator, and then returns to the office. Each "bathroom break" can take up to 15 minutes to complete. This is in addition to the occasional personal phone call received, casual office conversations, and informal chats that occur in a work environment.

But this is not Sergio's only apprehension. Additionally, because Sandy is visible in the lesbian, gay, bisexual, and transgender community, Sandy frequently gets phone calls for activism. It may be a reporter, it may be a community agency requesting a presentation, or it may be another personal request of some kind. The phone calls are not consistent, and they sometimes last briefly while other times require a longer conversation.

Finally, because of the physical transition from F to M (hormone treatments; medical evaluation; and preparation for reassignment surgery), Sandy is absent with occasional doctor's appointments. Sometimes these will be a morning appointment or sometimes Sandy requests to leave work early. There are also times Sandy is out for the day. While Sandy has accumulated sick leave, the absences are infrequent and irregular enough, but consistent enough, that Sergio believes it has impacted the workflow of the office he manages because he cannot plan for regularity. Due to budget restrictions, Sergio is not able to hire temporary employees.

Sergio spoke with one of Sandy's previous supervisors who had experienced similar issues and concerns with no resolution. When Sergio discussed similar concerns with Sandy in the past, Sandy argued that the union permits particular breaks during the day. Sandy further pointed out that lunch hours are often shortened to make up for time away from the desk during the day. Sergio's point is that time away from the desk is not regulated or consistent, and so it is difficult to count on Sandy's presence. Sandy retorted that one couldn't control the need to use the washroom, deal with a professional service request, or regulate one's physical body and health.

As Sergio prepares this year's evaluation, he does not feel that there has been any change in Sandy's awareness of out-of-the-office timing. He does not want a repeat exchange of last year's interaction. While he is trying to be sensitive to Sandy's transgender issues and concerns, he believes he has an office to run and Sandy's performance is not up to par, primarily because of the frequent momentary absences and sporadic sick leave. Yet, Sergio has come to believe there is a fine line between supporting Sandy and being taken advantage of in the workplace.

General Question:

1. How should Sergio best prepare for Sandy's performance evaluation?

Discussion Questions:

1. Do you think that Sergio should involve one of Sandy's union representatives? Why or why not?
2. Do you think Sergio should consult with a human resources representative? What is the role of human resources in this case?
3. Is Sergio being insensitive to Sandy's unique needs? Why? What could Sergio require of Sandy to make sure Sandy is there for him when he needs direct assistance?
4. Do you think Sergio should require medical verification on all of Sandy's absences and, if provided, simply adhere to Sandy's needs?

5. What role do you think gender in the workplace plays in this situation?

6. Do you think this scenario would unfold differently if Sandy were a F to M? Why or why not?

Case prepared by Patrick Finnessy, PhD, of the University of Toronto in Toronto, ON.

WORK/LIFE ISSUES

Case: What Is a Family?

Case: The Best Fit

Case: What Is A Family?

Organizational Policy and Discretionary Decisions: The Issue of Traditional Versus Nontraditional Family Structures

Candace Albright works at a branch campus for a large university known for its positive work environment and policies, which address the needs of the diverse workforce it employs. Candace recently suffered the loss of her stepfather. She went through all of the appropriate protocols, requesting bereavement leave to help her mother make funeral arrangements, attend the funeral, and deal with estate issues.

However, when the paperwork finally reached HR, the representative required her to take vacation days or unpaid leave because this man was not her biological father and thus not an immediate family member. Candace argued that he has actively raised her since the time she was 10 years old, providing emotional and financial support once he married her mother. These things make him an immediate family member even though he was not her biological father. When Candace continued to explain her son considers him his grandfather, the HR representative responded with "well, what will you do when your biological father dies"?

Candace was appalled by the insensitive response and treatment by this HR representative who would not allow her to use bereavement leave for the death of her stepfather, essentially making her choose between her biological father and her stepfather who equally raised her. She felt discriminated against because she was not part of a traditional nuclear family—even though the divorce rate in the United States is over 50% and over 60% of those with children remarry, thus creating stepparents who care for children that are not biologically theirs. It appears that the interpretation of who is and who is not an immediate family member has been left to the discretion of the HR representative handling the claim. Candace has the full support of her immediate supervisor, who feels that stepparents are immediate family members and therefore should be included when in need of using bereavement policies. However, she is unsure of what steps to take next, or if it is even worth the fight.

Case Resources:

- Sample HR Policy
  - Up to 5 working days of sick leave can be used in the death of an immediate family member. To obtain a bereavement leave an employee must complete and submit a leave form in addition to presenting an obituary or death certificate.

Definition of Immediate Family Member

- Immediate family members include: one's parents, stepparents, siblings, spouse, children, stepchildren, foster children, in-laws, sibling in-laws, grandparents, great grandparents, stepgreat grandparents, grandchildren, aunts, uncles, nieces, and nephews (Source: http://dictionary.reference.com/browse/immediate+family).

Discussion Questions:

1. How does an organization determine who an immediate family member is? If the criteria is a biological connection what happens in the case of a husband and wife, an adopted or foster child, or partners living together for twenty years?
2. Should stepparents be considered the same as biological parents? How should parental status be determined (e.g., by biology, monetary, or emotional support)?
3. How might this issue be translated differently if Candace's mother were a lesbian and the "stepfather" were instead her mother's female partner and co-parent to Candace? Should the situation be treated differently if Candace had never known her biological father?
4. Should Candace fight the decision? To whom should she take her case?
5. Were the HR representative's actions appropriate? How would you have handled this request if you were the HR representative? How much should Candace be required to disclose? At what point is the HR representative too intrusive?
6. What are your organizational policies on sick and bereavement leave? Are your organizations policies adequate or inadequate? What would you do to improve them?

Case prepared by Sunny Munn of Ohio State University in Columbus, OH, and Tonette Rocco, PhD, of Florida International University in Miami, FL.

Case: The Best Fit

Linda Evans is the vice president of human resources for a multinational fast food company headquartered in the United States. Evans sees herself as an open-minded, straight White female; after all, she loved watching the television show "Will and Grace," a sitcom that featured as protagonists a gay male and his best friend—a heterosexual woman. She is proud of her efforts to recruit and retain a diverse workforce and establish policies that help the company move beyond compliance with federal laws.

The company has offices in various countries in the European Union, the Caribbean, and North America. Over several years the company has developed and instituted a career development program designed to provide high-potential executives with a series of experiences at different levels, in each region, and under the guidance of a mentor. Two employees are coming up for a rotation in the Caribbean: Michael Crandle, an openly gay man, and Bella Pensera, a woman who might be a lesbian. The locations for the placement options are Jamaica, Bermuda, and Grenada. Linda has heard that some countries in the region promote mob violence against sexual minorities and have laws making homosexuality a crime punishable by prison time. She can't believe this is true.

Discussion Questions:

1. What are the laws that prohibit employment discrimination on the basis of sexual orientation?
2. What efforts can a company take to champion employee diversity, including sexual orientation and gender identity? What are the differences between compliance with laws that prohibit discrimination and efforts to champion and leverage diversity?
3. What should Evans consider before placing Crandle and Pensera in their executive development assignments?
4. Does the location of those assignments matter, given the sexual orientation of these two high-potential employees? Explain.

Case prepared by Tonette Rocco, PhD, of Florida International University in Miami, FL, Julie Gedro, EdD, of Empire State College in Syracuse, NY, and Martin Kormanik, PhD, of O.D. Systems in Alexandria, VA.

MANAGEMENT DEVELOPMENT

Activity: Leading the Way

Case: The New Manager

Activity: Leading the Way

Introduction

A very important skill in the field of adult education and training is to be able to design and develop educational programs from multiple perspectives. Merriam, Caffarella, and Baumgartner (2007) compare and contrast the behavioral, humanistic, social, cognitive, and constructivist learning orientations. The following case is designed to assist you in developing skills in designing adult education and training programs from these varied perspectives.

The Case

You are the human resource trainer at a medium-sized technology and data management company. In your company, it is typical for those individuals who are good technicians or experts in development of software, or systems analysts to get promoted to management and leadership positions. Most often these individuals have no prior experience in leadership or management. They enter their new management position with outstanding technical skills, but a lack of skills in communication, budgeting, supervision, and general leadership. The company has decided that technicians who are promoted need to undergo leadership training and has asked you to develop the program.

Discussion Questions:

1. How would you develop this training program from a humanistic perspective?

   Outline the following for your program:

   - Needs assessment
   - Program design
   - Program objectives
   - Learning activities
   - Evaluation strategies

2. How would you develop this training program from a behavioral perspective?

   Outline the following for your program:

   - Needs assessment
   - Program design

- Program objectives
- Learning activities
- Evaluation strategies

3. How would you develop this training program from a constructivist perspective?

   Outline the following for your program:

   - Needs assessment
   - Program design
   - Program objectives
   - Learning activities
   - Evaluation strategies

4. How would you develop this training program from a social learning perspective?

   Outline the following for your program:

   - Needs assessment
   - Program design
   - Program objectives
   - Learning activities
   - Evaluation strategies

REFERENCE

Merriam, S. B., Caffarella, R. S., & Baumgartner, L. (2007). *Learning in adulthood* (3rd ed.). San Francisco, CA: Jossey-Bass.

Activity prepared by Barbara J. Daley, PhD, of the University of Wisconsin–Milwaukee, in Milwaukee, WI.

Case: The New Manager

James, a machine operator, was recently promoted to general manager of the small manufacturing company where he has worked for over 20 years. The people he now supervises are his longtime friends, coworkers, and some were even members of his family. After only a brief time on the job, James found himself in the peculiar position of having to make some tough decisions.

When Debbie, a coworker of his for over 10 years, began to miss work, take longer breaks, and her productivity was noticeably lower, James had to address these issues with her. This was tough for James because he has been friends with her for a long time, has met her family, and has even eaten at her home. However, at this time, James was not a friend and coworker, but rather a supervisor and possibly a disciplinarian.

James was experiencing a very classic case of "role conflict." He was in a situation in which incompatible role demands were placed on him by two statuses held at the same time—"friend" and "boss," Torn with exactly how to handle the situation, James decided that he must uphold company policies related to work behavior, and he gave Debbie a formal written reprimand.

Having won even more favor with his superiors by acting in the best interest of the company, James realizes he has quite possibly lost a long-time friend. He quickly comes to the realization that this is a situation that he may face over and over, and he needs some way of dealing with it positively. His dilemma is overwhelming. He wants to be a good friend and a good manager at the same time.

Having had no previous management training, James approaches the two-person human resources staff and asks if there is any management training that he can attend that will help him adjust to his new role in the company. He is told because of the present economic pitfalls, there is no budget for management training, and that they hope to have training for new managers some day. With this information, James realizes it is all up to him to equip himself with the skills necessary to become a people manager.

James figures that he has several options, among which are enrolling in the local community college and taking business classes, paying for high-priced seminars, or just struggling along and "learning the ropes" as best he can. He considers that the first two options are constraints on his time and money, especially with his new responsibilities at work. On the other hand, he feels that he can't wait for the organization to tell him when he can learn. James concludes that he will have to take charge of his learning situation and become a self-directed learner.

General Question:

1. Whose responsibility is management development? How much of the development of managerial skills is left to managers themselves?

Discussion Questions:

1. If you were in James's position, how would you go about developing your managerial skills?
2. Given his time and money constraints, what are some possible opportunities for learning that James could take advantage of in this situation?
3. Even in a budget "pitfall," what could human resources have done to support James?
4. What are the specific characteristics of self-directed learning which will be the most helpful to James in his challenge?
5. How important is self-directed learning in today's workplace for managers and all employees to gain the competitive advantage?

Case prepared by Thomas Cox, EdD, of the University of Houston–Victoria, in Victoria, TX.

ETHICS IN ADULT EDUCATION
AND HUMAN RESOURCE DEVELOPMENT

Activity: Ethics in Human Resource Development

Case: A Trainer's Dilemma

Case: Safety or Security First?

Activity: Ethics in Human Resource Development

The Academy of Human Resource Development (AHRD) is a premier organization in the field of human resource development (HRD). Access the Academy of Human Resource Development's website at www.ahrd.org, and locate their Standards on Ethics and Integrity.

1. If you work in the field of HRD, consider your own position. If you do not, consider an HRD position to which you aspire, or one with which you are familiar.
2. If you an HRD practitioner, what types of HRD-related ethical issues have you been faced with? How did you handle them? Do the AHRD's Standards on Ethics and Integrity address those same issues in any way?
3. If you are planning a career in HRD, what types of HRD-related ethical issues might you be faced with?
4. If you are conducting research in the field of HRD for a thesis or dissertation, for example, what types of ethical issues must you be aware of?

Activity prepared by Steven W. Schmidt, PhD, of East Carolina University in Greenville, NC.

Case: A Trainer's Dilemma

Food Staples is a family-owned grocery store chain in the state of Midland. The first grocery store in the chain was opened in 1929 by Theodore Dont. Since that time, Food Staples has remained family owned and has expanded to a total of 48 stores in the state of Midland. Theodore Dont, the Food Staples founder, was a generous and philanthropic man who contributed his time and financial resources to many worthy causes that benefited the people of Midland. Further, Theodore Dont instilled a sense of philanthropy in his two sons, both of whom are now running the Food Staples enterprise since their father retired. The Dont family has come to be known as an upstanding family in the state of Midland and despite having opportunities to expand beyond Midland, the family has elected to keep its stores within the confines of Midland. Recently Good Foods and other national grocery store chains have entered the Midland marketplace. Midland has retained its customer base but the buzz in Midland is that that the new grocery store chains in comparison to Food Staples are offering a fresh perspective on grocery shopping and a hallmark characteristic of grocery shopping at these stores is superb customer service.

Harry Dont, the chief executive officer of Food Staples and his brother Sam, the vice president of operations, heard about the contrasting experiences of customers shopping in Food Staples stores and those shopping in the new national chain grocery stores and decided to improve customer service within Food Staples. You have been contracted with the Donts to do a needs assessment to find out what types of customer services training is needed for in-store personnel (cashiers and store clerks). In your scope of work document you propose to use surveys and randomly selected interviews with in-store personnel at stores located across the state of Midland. In one of your preliminary data gathering interviews, a twenty-something woman of Mexican ancestry with poor English speaking skills, asks if the interview was confidential. You inform her that it is confidential. Based upon this understanding, they young woman proceeds to tell you about incidents of sexual harassment against her by a vice president and family member owner of the Food Staples grocery chain. The young woman concludes her story by asking for assurances that the information she provided would be kept confidential. Furthermore, In the process of conducting additional preliminary interviews with other in-store employees, you hear similar stories of sexual harassment from two other young immigrant women at different stores.

General Question:

1. Given that you contracted to do a needs assessment for identifying customer service training, would you proceed with the needs assessment in light of the sexual harassment information presented to you?

Discussion Questions:

1. What types of issues present in this situation?
2. Are there vulnerable stakeholders in this situation? Explain.
3. What personal, moral and ethical standards would you use to guide your actions in this situation?
4. Do you feel obligated to bring this issue to the owners of Food Staples?

Case prepared by Ray K. Haynes, PhD, of Indiana University in Bloomington, IN.

Case: Safety or Security First?

In a large military-industrial complex, a significant number of employees were under serious threat of being laid off, terminated, or relocated due to automation of the work they had previously been performing. In an effort to retain some of the employees, they were given the option of retraining for more hazardous, but critical HAZMAT work. Such work involves the chemical identification, spill containment, clean-up, and removal of any variety of hazardous materials within the massive complex. Although the training required would be time-consuming and costly, the advantages to the company to such cross-training were significant in terms of improved public relations and employee morale, savings in severance packages and unemployment costs, and reductions in new employee orientation and training expenses, which would not be required for existing employees. Additionally, the reclassified employees could be trained and placed in entry-level positions in the hazardous field at lower salaries than would be needed to hire others in the field.

Employees were counseled regarding the severity of threat to their existing jobs, given promotional literature about the new career field, advised about the advantages of the work (in terms of stability, higher salaries, ongoing professional training and education, and certification), and provided with an outline of the extensive training required. The company agreed to continue the current (lower) salaries during the 8-weeks of required training. Once employees successfully completed the required training and passed both the practical exercises and final examinations, they would be allowed to pursue certification testing—after which they would be reclassified and moved to their new positions. Of the approximately 50 individuals who were threatened with the loss of their current jobs, 28 chose to apply for the new positions and training opportunity and new positions.

Training was contracted to a private human development management firm, and begun, first in onsite classroom space, then in remote and vacated locations in the complex for the applied practice and testing. The training team consisted of subject matter experts (SMEs), trainers and developers, instructional design specialists, and evaluation experts. Not only were the consultants all skilled and experienced in training design and implementation; several of them were certified in hazardous materials identification, containment, and removal with years of experience and knowledge of the many hazards.

Approximately 3 weeks into the classroom training, one of the trainers overheard an excited but troubled conversation among a group of women employees—conversation that focused on the unexpected joy of one of the women who had just learned she was pregnant. As the trainer listened quietly from the hallway, the conversation included the soon-to-be mother's mixed emotions about her new pregnancy. She would be a single mother, badly in need of a better job with more stability and more income. She was otherwise healthy except for the health risks to both her health and that of her unborn child from the chemicals that she could potentially come into contact with. She wondered if, when, and even to whom she might confide in about her pregnancy and concerns for the potential hazards to her unborn child. Her coworkers alternately advised her "to keep quiet about it" or that she "had to quit right away." Speculations arose among them about the early stage of pregnancy she would reach before completing the training and having the necessary certification; about the possibility that she would be terminated from the training should management discover her pregnancy; and about the degree to which she would be able to refrain in the future from any truly dangerous chemical exposure. Already in their studies, the women had learned that exposure to some chemicals were especially potentially harmful in the earliest stages of pregnancy. All female trainees had signed affidavits that they were, in fact, not pregnant at the time the training started.

Discussion Questions:

1. Knowing of the promise of better employment and higher salaries, albeit it with increased risks, might the female employee already have conceived prior to starting the training?

2. What is her obligation to her own health, that of her unborn child, or employer?

3. Can the company allow the woman to finish the training safely without the hands-on application and testing with actual hazardous chemicals? Should this be allowed or could it result in a less qualified and safely trained individual?

4. Should the trainer confront the women with the knowledge of her conversation? Should the trainer tell someone else on the training team or management?

5. What are the ethical dilemmas embedded in this complex human interaction.

Case prepared by Vivian Mott, PhD, of East Carolina University in Greenville, NC.

INTERNATIONAL HUMAN RESOURCE DEVELOPMENT

Case: Cross-Cultural Fatigue

Case: Cross-Cultural Fatigue

Iris Smith was sitting in her Shanghai office and thinking of the emergent issue that might threaten her company's image and reputation. She was very exhausted and she felt panicked and confused.

It had never been a hard decision for Iris to accept the overseas assignment. She was single and loved travel and challenging jobs. She grew up in Boston, and due to her history major in college, had developed a strong interest in ancient Chinese history. She even participated in an international exchanged program for one summer in China when she was a junior. In the program, she had learned some Mandarin. This experience had contributed to her career aspiration with Mesco, the largest retailing business in the United States.

Iris had worked 6 years as an associate manager for public relations at the Mesco headquarters. She was recognized as an efficient, ambitious, and determined manager by the top management of Mesco. Iris was promoted to take an overseas assignment managing public relations for the first Masco Chinese subsidiary in Shanghai. Iris's Chinese experience and background were a big plus for her in the selection process.

Based on Iris's Chinese background, Mesco only gave her a 1-day cultural briefing workshop as a predeparture training. In the morning session, the trainer introduced modern history and cultural background on China. In the afternoon, the trainer and Iris communicated in Mandarin, and the trainer prepared a daily Mandarin communication booklet for Iris to check and practice after the training session.

Although Mesco did arrange the relocation for Iris, there was no other training for her. The first month of her arrival in Shanghai was very challenging; however, everything was interesting to her. Iris worked to understand more about Chinese to make the transition successful. After 2 months she started to enjoy aspects of her new life in Shanghai. Only two things made Iris feel uncomfortable: so many people who smoked in public places and the traffic problems in the main streets. In her mind, she knew that she was an American in China now. In the Shanghai's office, there were five expatriates including Iris. She was the only female expatriate manager. Iris normally did not hang out with the American managers or Chinese managers after work. She tried to keep her professional and private lives separate.

After 6 months, Iris concluded that there were many different processes, business practices, and conflict solutions between Chinese and American cultures. Her American colleagues expected Iris to understand and communicate with local managers in Mandarin without any misunderstandings, and to deal with the local government officials without any disagreements. Iris began to realize that her Mandarin and Chinese knowledge were just not enough. She wished she had some good local friends to help her with her language skills and cultural understanding. At the same time, Iris started to more frequently miss her family members and friends in the United States.

There was one thing that made Iris really feel upset, and that was the feeling of gender discrimination. Iris often felt both Chinese and American male managers ignored her ideas in meetings. She felt pressure to prove her competence in front of her new colleagues. The hardest thing for her was to understand the Chinese concept of "Guang-Xi"; the Chinese way of building connections and relationships with colleagues, clients, customers, and local government officials.

Recently, there was a crisis that threatened Mesco's image in Shanghai. The local news reported that many customers went to hospital emergency rooms on Sunday after eating beef, which they bought from Mesco. The story was picked up and repeated by many news outlets. The Mesco corporate office in the United States required that Iris take immediate action to save Mesco's reputation in China. Having been there only 6 months, and still in the transition process, she was tired, confused, and wondering how to deal with this issue. She was now sitting in her office and thinking strategically about the next step she should take.

Discussion Questions:

1. If you were Iris, what steps would you take in managing this urgent case?

2. Did Mesco's Human Resource Department select the right person (Iris) for the overseas assignment?

3. What do you think of Iris's cross-cultural training workshop? Would you offer any modifications for it?

4. What advise would you give Iris to help her ease her cross-cultural fatigue?

5.   What advise would you give Iris regarding the gender discrimination she is feeling?

6. What processes and practices do you suggest for Mesco in selecting, training, developing expatriates?

Case submitted by Pi-Chi Han, EdD, of the University of Missouri–St. Louis in St. Louis, MO.

THE ADULT LEARNER

Case: The Online Learner

Case: Back to School

Case: The Move to Online Learning

Case: The Online Learner

Joe was enrolled in his first online education course at State University, and was enjoying the experience a great deal. Until the adult education program at State started offering courses online, he was not able to take courses at all, as the university's campus was about an hour from where he lived. Making that drive to class would have been impossible with all of Joe's other responsibilities, which included his job and his family. The course in which Joe was enrolled was an introduction to adult education course that featured synchronous chat sessions twice per week, asynchronous discussion boards, a variety of readings, a group project, and several written assignments. Joe thought that the instructor was good at teaching online, and used a variety of methods to engage learners.

One of the things the instructor did during the first unit of class was to have all learners post information about themselves on a "Get to Know You" discussion board. Learners were encouraged to post pictures or video clips of themselves as well. Through this forum, Joe learned that someone from his own town was also a student in the class. Like Joe, this was Alice's first experience with online learning, and she too was in this class because the drive to State University would have been prohibitive. Joe and Alice had communicated online several times when they found out they lived in the same city, and they had gotten to know each other through this online communication.

About halfway through the semester, Joe got an e-mail message from Alice. "How are you doing in class, Joe?", read Alice's message. "I'm having some difficulty with things. This online learning experience is not what I thought it would be. I feel like I'm here all alone, typing words into a computer. I don't feel like I'm being taught anything, and I don't feel connected to the class or the university at all. Maybe taking courses online is not for me."

Discussion Questions:

1. If you were Joe, how would you respond to Alice's message?
2. What advice might you give Alice?
3. What additional information from Alice would you want to know?
4. What is the responsibility of the learner in this case?

Case prepared by Steven W. Schmidt, PhD, of East Carolina University in Greenville, NC.

Case: Back to School

Five years after retiring, Edna's life circumstances had changed dramatically. Faced with rising costs of living and a retirement diminished by the economic recession, Edna decided to take her relative good health, determination, and drive back into the workforce. Edna was recently widowed and relied on social security and a small pension to pay her bills. While looking to earn additional income, Edna found that even part-time work in nearly every job she interviewed for required basic computer literacy and skills. Edna was a 65-year-old woman who had retired from her position after 30 years as an office manager for a small, private business. She went to high school in an era well before the common use of computer technologies. While on the job she had been trained on the use of typewriters, shorthand, professional courtesy and communication, file management, and conventional adding machines from other staff.

During the 1980s and 1990s, the office where Edna worked had been managed via manual, paper-based procedures and techniques. As personal computers made their way into mainstream society by the early 1990s, Edna did not believe that she needed to learn computers because of her approaching retirement. She saw computers as a tool for work use, not personal use, so she did not purchase one for her home. She felt that the steep learning curve was a poor investment of time and that the younger staff members would be better suited for computer-related office work. She did remain abreast of new innovations in the technologies she was already acquainted with such as typewriters, copy machines, and fax machines.

Edna realized that computer literacy was a gap in her skill set and she not only needed these skills to be competent in any job, she also needed these skills in order to be a part of a high-tech society. Given her situation, Edna decided to return to school so that she could learn computer skills at a local college. Edna's decision to seek training at the college level left her feeling nervous and anxious. She feared that she would not be able to keep up with the pace or the material. Edna normally had plenty of self-confidence because of the many achievements she had accomplished throughout her life. She had worked a job for 30 years, been married and raised a family, and had been an active member of her community. However, as she contemplated being in the classroom with students in their teens and twenties, the idea of learning new technologies was frightening. She feared feeling embarrassed by her lack of knowledge and her apparent lack of skills. She expected younger students to stare, laugh, and possibly even verbally criticize her as she tried to learn. Edna did not personally own a computer or have anyone in her close personal circle who could give her help outside of class.

Once class began, Edna showed up each day before class and would review and study the course content and readings. The instructor would lecture, demonstrate computer skills, and then ask students to repeat the skills he demonstrated. She sat in the front row of the class, directly in front of the instructor and would take notes as the instructor would teach. During hands-on activities, she would sit and observe or sit and write notes detailing the exercise. Edna would not ask questions or attempt to replicate any of the computer skills during class. Each day near the end of class, Edna would ask the instructor to stay after the other students were dismissed. During this time she would ask a myriad of questions that she had written down during the class period. She would also ask the instructor for a repeat demonstration of all of the skills she had seen the instructor perform during the class. In essence, Edna would sit in class and then spend about 20 minutes of time outside of class with the instructor each day to personally receive the one-on-one instruction needed to help her understand the concepts of the course. The instructor felt that he was reteaching the course content, but Edna appeared to have a high level of satisfaction from the independent tutoring, and would state that each session made her feel more comfortable with the material.

After 2 weeks of attending class and having after class sessions, Edna had her first assignment to complete for submission and grading. The after-class sessions were helpful to her, but when forced to work independently on an assignment, she had difficulty remembering the steps and directions covered in class. While trying to complete the assignment, she felt confused and frustrated. She tried to follow the directions using the computer software but was eventually unable to complete the assignment. Feeling embarrassed, she did not turn in her assignment at all. During the next class period, Edna sat quietly unengaged at her desk. The instructor noticed that she did not make much eye contact or take notes as frequently as before, and would not touch the mouse and keyboard unless he was near her desk. After class, she did not immediately request a one-on-one session with the instructor. The instructor noticed these changes in her behavior and sensed a problem. The instructor checked and also realized that she had not submitted her assignment. During the next class period, the instructor asked Edna about her assignment and her progress in general. Edna told the instructor about her feelings and that she was contemplating dropping the class.

She made statements about how difficult it was for her to keep up with other students and about how she wasn't as quick as she once was. She also stated that while in class, she had a hard time with the pace of the instructor and the other students, and that she needed more time to take notes and study before attempting the computer skills which were being demonstrated.

The instructor was perplexed with this situation and was unsure about what to do for Edna. Prior to this conversation, and based on other after-class meetings, he thought Edna was doing well. He was unsure about which actions to take, but encouraged Edna to stick with the class until he could consider the situation more carefully and give her more direct guidance.

General Question:

1. As a technology instructor, how would you approach a student like Edna? What are Edna's challenges? What type of instructional interventions would you employ in order to help her succeed? Would your behaviors, words, teaching strategies, assignments or evaluations be different for this student? If not, why? If yes, exactly what would you do differently for this student?

Discussion Questions:

1. What can Edna do outside of class to help her improve her success in school?
2. What study strategies would you suggest Edna use to assist her in learning to use new technologies?
3. How can the theories of motivation and learning be used to enhance the abilities of adult learners like Edna?
4. To what extent do you think the role of self-efficacy played in Edna's performance?
5. What (if any) impact does Edna's age have on her ability to learn computer technology from an **emotional** and **social** perspective?
6. What (if any) impact does Edna's age have on her ability to learn computer technology from a **physiological** perspective?
7. Did Edna have any bias or negative beliefs that affected her own performance? If so, identify these beliefs and bias.
8. How did Edna's past work experiences affect her learning of new, modern technologies?
9. Why would Edna wait to ask all of her questions after class?
10. What is the instructor's role in this situation?

11. How would you, as an instructor, feel if you had a student like Edna who waited until after class to ask questions?

Case prepared by Jeremy Dickerson, EdD, and Shelia Tucker, PhD, both of East Carolina University in Greenville, NC.

Case: The Move to Online Learning

John Miller works for Hanson-Dean Pharmaco, a small pharmaceutical company. He has worked there for the last 4 years as an instructional systems specialist in the training department. In his position, John develops instructional programs and conducts traditional face-to-face training sessions. Hanson-Dean Pharmaco is under new management and has a new training director. That new training director, Bill Spencer, is interested in offering more online training opportunities for employees. Hanson-Dean Pharmaco has offered online training in the past, but outsources all of its online training.

Bill is a firm believer in online training. He believes the time has come to decrease the outsourcing of online training and move that function in house. He wants John to lead that effort, and instructs John to use available and accessible resources on the Internet.

Bill wants John to start developing online courses for the company's regional sales managers, focusing on the areas of coaching, conflict resolution, and team building. Bill has stated that there is a small amount of funds for additional resources. He believes this online format will show a positive return on investment.

John is aware of the challenges of developing online courses. He is aware that this new focus poses challenges not only to the mangers but to the Hanson-Dean Pharmaco training department as well. He is excited about the opportunity to developing online training.

General Question:

1. What are some important aspects of adult learning that John should be considering as he moves forward with this initiative?

Discussion Questions:

1. What are the advantages and disadvantages of online training in this case?
2. What are some principles of effective online training?
3. How do effective adult education facilitation and principles of effective online training relate to each other?
4. What about the learners (regional sales managers) would John need to know in order to develop these online courses?

5. What are some effective adult education facilitation methods John may consider employing in the teaching of these topics (coaching, conflict resolution, and team building) to regional sales managers? What types of qualifications should facilitators for these courses posses?

Case prepared by Kenneth D. Ott, EdD, of Valdosta State University in Valdosta, GA.

GENERAL CLASSROOM ACTIVITIES

Information: Overview and Activity Guidelines

Activities: Future Back Vision
Table Buzz
Class Challenges
Mind Mapping to Solve Problems
Breaking News Exercise
Choose Your Words
Spreading the News
Reflection for Question Time

Overview and Activity Guidelines

Time-intensive courses are prevalent in many settings. In academia where adult learner programs exist, coursework may involve meeting once a week for 3 to 4 hours for multiple sessions. In the corporate world, training sessions are frequently geared to half-day or full-day sessions where attendees are expected to be engaged in learning activities for up to 4 to 8 hours.

Facilitators, teachers, or trainers of time-intensive courses must employ a variety of tools to communicate material and encourage critical thinking. One critical component to a successful time-intensive course is to create an agenda ahead of time that is segmented into time increments using multiple learning strategies. No one learning tool should exceed 45 minutes.

One way to organize time-intensive courses is with a 15-minute lecture/discussion followed by a specific instructional technique that reinforces the material covered. Using local market, business, or education-related situations helps illustrate why the problem matters to the students and the community. Outlined below are useful tools and techniques that can be woven into time-intensive adult learner classes or training sessions. Many of the examples and specifics noted in these exercises deal with human resources, but they can be used with many other course topics.

Introduction contributed by Denise Cumberland of YUM Brands and Spalding University; both in Louisville, KY.

Activity: Future Back Vision

In the first class students are asked to develop a future back vision around a specific human resource question. Typically this is prework the student writes prior to class. At the onset of the class students form teams of two, introduce themselves to each other and share their answers with their partner. Next we spend time having each team introduce one another and provide headlines about that persons' future back vision on that specific question. Example questions include:

- Describe what the future of HR looks like for an employee 10 years from now?
- If you were promoted tomorrow to be the head of HR, what would you change in your company? Why?

Adaptation for online courses for "Future Back Vision" is possible by having students introduce themselves with an autobiographical statement in an online discussion board. As part of that autobiographical statement students must also answer one of the above questions. Each student is required to read about one other student and comment on that student's answer to the question. In order to ensure each student's work is read, the student must locate someone in the class whose autobiography has not previously been commented upon.

Activity contributed by Denise Cumberland of YUM Brands and Spalding University; both in Louisville, KY.

Activity: Table Buzz

Table Buzz is an opportunity for a group of three to four students to engage in brainstorming on a specific human resource issue. Each team is given a different situation. The theme of each situation is based on the reading material and in class lecture/discussion. Each team reflects on the lecture and readings and outlines an action plan for addressing the issue. An example is shared below.

- Assumption: You are employed as a human resource specialist for Memorial East Hospital in Jamesville. Your boss, the chief people officer (CPO) is concerned because retention among nurses has declined for the past 4 years. The healthcare market in Jamesville is exceptionally competitive with Norton Hospital adding a new addition, as well as continual competition from Jewish Hospital. The CPO decides that your main task over the next 30 days is to develop a retention program for the nursing staff. She wants to review the outline of your action plan by tomorrow. Objective for students: as a team determine what is a solid action plan to present to the CPO in 24 hours. Remember, the action plan will outline the steps you will take over the next 30 days to deliver a world class retention program for the nursing staff at Memorial East Hospital.

An online program may turn Table Buzz into "Chat Buzz." Multiple situations can be posted online where students opt into a specific group. Each group works together in an online chat room to create an action plan for accomplishing the objectives. A 30- to 45-minute chat sessions should allow each group to create and post a solid action plan to present to the CPO.

Activity contributed by Denise Cumberland of YUM Brands and Spalding University; both in Louisville, KY.

Activity: Class Challenges

In class challenge, teams are formed and play against each other using a series of time based questions. The format is "Jeopardy" style, with the instructor acting as the emcee or host. The objective for Class Challenges is to ensure specific "facts" that the student must know are repeated under intense circumstances. Using a competitive context can create neuron fire power that creates "stickiness" around the terms and definitions. Examples of questions are shown below.

- What does the acronym POWER hiring stand for? (Performance profiles, Objective Evaluations, Wide Range Sourcing, Emotional Control, Recruiting Effectiveness)
- What are SMART objectives for team member performance goals? (Specific, Measureable, Action Oriented, Result Focused, Time Bound)

Activity contributed by Denise Cumberland of YUM Brands and Spalding University; both in Louisville, KY.

Activity: Mind Mapping to Solve Problems

In this exercise students are the taught how to "mind map" an issue. The activity is designed to ensure students are learning to formulate new ideas in human resource management or any other discipline. By teaching how to mind map students are given a new tool that facilitates creating new ideas

- **Example Topic**: How can our company promote stronger work life balance for employees?
- **Structure:** Students are requested to bring in a picture of what stresses them out and a picture of what makes them happy. Students are then divided into groups of four and they share why they chose those pictures. Then each group creates a "pain pile" and a "pleasure pile." Next each group is assigned one of the piles to create a mind map. The pain pile or the pleasure pile is mapped and

the students map ideas on how a company could eliminate the pain or enhance the pleasure. Teams then present their mind map and other teams must provide commentary.

Activity contributed by Denise Cumberland of YUM Brands and Spalding University; both in Louisville, KY.

Activity: Breaking News Exercise

This exercise involves role playing to reinforce the material covered in class. The object is to ensure the students can analyze a specific topic objectively.

- **Example Topic:** A press release has been issued by McDonald's Restaurants that their human resource team has created an online learning tool that will reduce team member training costs by 75% and improve order accuracy.
- **Structure:** Each member of class is either a "journalist from Business Week" or the "chief people officer" for McDonald's. Each is given 7 minutes to prepare for the interview. The mock journalist must formulate questions that would enable them to write a news story. The chief people officer must be able to provide answers on why this online learning tool is revolutionary.

Activity contributed by Denise Cumberland of YUM Brands and Spalding University; both in Louisville, KY.

Activity: Choose Your Words

To illustrate the importance of words and how powerful they can be in dealing with people, the class is charged with substituting new words at the beginning of every session. The "initial" word can be positive or negative. Throughout the session of the evening we go back to each word and if the word is positive, we make it more powerful by "upping the ante." If the word is negative we try and lessen the intensity. Examples:

- Fearful to Curious/Uncomfortable
- Frustrated to Challenged/Delayed

- Hurt to Bothered/Ruffled
- Focused to Energized/Intensity
- Energized to Turbo-Charged/On Fire
- Determined to Unstoppable/Fearless

Activity contributed by Denise Cumberland of YUM Brands and Spalding University; both in Louisville, KY.

Activity: Spreading the News

In order to emphasize the importance of communication and how to evaluate different communication approaches, the next exercise is conducted in teams. A human resource announcement (for example) is given to a team. The team must determine how to communicate the message to a specific group of employees. This task requires students to think about how to contextualize the message to a certain group, as well as asses what would be the best mechanism to communicate the information. Each team is given 10 minutes to formulate their communication plan. The cards are collected. Students then critique the plan and note what was effective and what could have been more effective. An example of a topic is as follows:

- In the purchasing department of a major manufacturing company, the vice president of purchasing and materials management has decided that all buyers must attain a national certification if they are to continue in their positions. Certification involves passing a series of tests that are known to be somewhat rigorous. Purchasers in the department range in age from 25 to 65. Some of the younger employees have 4-year degrees, but many tenured employees have high school diplomas. Some of the more tenured employees have been in their positions for 30 years. Many have not been involved in formal educational programs for 30 years. The department has enlisted the help of human resource development professionals to help prepare for the series of tests.

Activity contributed by Denise Cumberland of YUM Brands and Spalding University; both in Louisville, KY.

Activity: Reflection for Question Time

In an extended class it's also critical to give students a chance to absorb the material at a slower pace that gives them the opportunity to think about the information and formulate questions. During "Reflection for Question Time" students are given 10 minutes to review the material discussed in the session. The students are required to write two thought-provoking questions. The questions don't necessarily have an answer, but should allow their classmates opportunity for discussion.

Activity contributed by Denise Cumberland of YUM Brands and Spalding University; both in Louisville, KY.

CHAPTER 4

WRITE YOUR
OWN CASE STUDY

Each reader's level of familiarity with the use of case studies is different. Regardless of your prior experience, this chapter will expand your expertise in the actual design and development of case studies. Practical guidance and examples are provided to enable you to create custom case studies for use in the classroom.

Perhaps you participated in case study exercises as a student or instructor, or maybe you've facilitated a case study discussion. You may have been exposed to the use of case studies as educational tools for many years, or this may be your first exposure to them. You might be a firm believer in the value of case studies or you may still be a skeptic. Maybe you were sold on the use of case studies after having read this book. If you used case studies in your classes, you may not have been familiar with the background information presented in the opening chapters of this book. Hopefully, those chapters provided additional insights that you've incorporated into the way you use case studies—as an instructor or a student.

If you have read this far in the book, you must have some interest in the use of case studies (either that, or the reading of these chapters was assigned and you've read this far because it was a requirement). Along the way, it is possible that you've had an "a-ha" moment or two in which you've recalled a situation that you believe would make a great case study. If you are an instructor, maybe you are considering having your

Case Studies and Activities in Adult Education and Human Resources Development
pp. 165–179
Copyright © 2010 by Information Age Publishing
All rights of reproduction in any form reserved.

students develop their own case studies as an assignment for one of your classes. Maybe you are a student who's been assigned to teach a course or facilitate a discussion in a particular subject, and you believe that a case study exercise would be an appropriate activity to include in your session. If any of these situations are true, this chapter is for you. It was developed to provide you with information on how to develop your own case study.

Let us review the types of case studies identified by Simmons (1974, cited in Armistead, 1984) in chapter 1. Those types are presented again below, and will be referenced throughout this section.

- **The exercise case study** provides an opportunity for the student to practice the application of specific procedures.
- **The situation case study** is the type most generally associated with the term case study. The student is asked to analyze the information in the case.
- **The complex case study** is an extension of the situation case study. The student is required to handle a large amount of data and information, some of which is irrelevant.
- **The decision case study** requires the student to go a step further than in the previous category and present plans for solving a problem.
- **The in-basket case study** is a particular type of decision case study. The student is presented with a collection of documents and background information and is expected to record the actions he or she would take relating to each document, some of which will be interrelated.
- **The critical incident case study** provides the student with a certain amount of information and withholds other information until it is requested by the student.
- **The action maze case study** presents a large case study in a series of small units. The student is required at each stage to predict what will happen next.
- **The role play case study** requires the student and perhaps the case leader to assume roles in the case (Simmons, 1974, cited in Armistead, 1984).

You do not have to start out knowing the type of case study you wish to develop. To some degree the type of story you choose to develop into a case study will influence the type of case study you write.

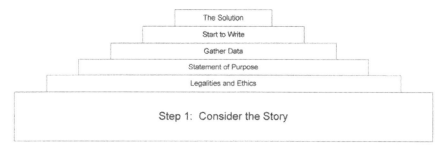

Figure 4.1.

STEP 1: CONSIDER THE STORY

As noted at the beginning of this book, case studies are basically stories that have been organized and presented in a format that allows them to be learning tools. The key is in the successful conversion of the story to the case study. As a first step, consider the story you intend to develop into a case study. Why would it make a good case study? It is important that you select a topic or story that is meaningful to you, or one in which you are interested, for the simple reason that you are more likely to complete a case study in which you are interested. It is also important that you have some knowledge in the area in which you are writing. Remember that issues like relevance and accuracy are important. It may be easy for authors to write case studies on topics with which they are not familiar, but that does not mean that those case studies will be effective for those students who are using them as learning tools. The best case studies are developed by people who know their subjects, and who are able to differentiate between important and unimportant details to present compelling and interesting scenarios for evaluation.

Carter (1999) believes that there are two reasons why stories become good case studies. They are either examples of exemplary practice or interesting problem situations.

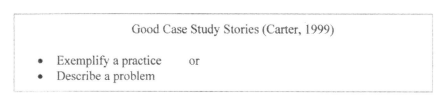

Figure 4.2.

Exemplary Stories

> One prominent use of cases is to illustrate a general category or to exemplify a practice. Such cases are commonly used in teacher preparation to depict vividly such matters as the complexity of teaching environments, the way in which a method is actually carried out in a classroom, or the complicated ways a general proposition about learning or development might manifest itself in concrete situations. (Carter, 1999, p. 166)

Exemplary cases are designed so that the student understands the complexity of the situation, the variables to be considered, and the course of action ultimately chosen. That does not necessarily mean that the action chosen was correct, and alternative paths (and their corresponding consequences and merits) may be discussed as well. In fact, the trial and error process of decision making taken by the characters in the case may be noted as part of the case study itself. Exemplary cases are appropriate when looking at details and making connections between those smaller details in play and the larger issues present. They help students to understand the weight, or importance given to each detail and the prioritization of those details when making decisions.

When developing an exemplary case, keep in mind that while details are important, not every detail has to be noted (although critical details should not be excluded). Exemplary cases must contain details, but there should not be so many details that readers become overwhelmed and tune out. Remember that the point of developing an exemplary case is to help the reader understand the course of action taken. The main topic that the author wishes to highlight will help to determine the details to include and those to omit.

Problem Situations

Problem situation-type cases are developed to help participants interpret data and make decisions based on those interpretations. "In contrast

	Ten Second Tip
	Knowledge of subject and the ability to discriminate between important and unimportant details are important when developing a case study.

Figure 4.3.

to exemplars, problem cases are often more complex and less well-formed representations of teaching" (Carter, 1999, p. 168). In the problem situation-type case, participants are given information and asked to solve a problem. Unlike exemplary cases, which typically contain information on the decisions chosen, problem situation cases are more focused on the presentation of information. They may not include information on the path chosen or the decisions made by the characters in the case. Rather, participants are required to bring their own knowledge related to the situation and the issue, and consider how they would solve the problem. Carter (1999) compares the exemplary and problem situation case studies as follows: "Rather than simply illustrating (like an exemplary case), a case as problem situation becomes a canvas on which various types of information are combined and arranged to resolve an issue or dilemma" (p. 167).

Consider developing an exemplary case if you have a complicated situation that you wish to describe. If you have a problem to be solved, the problem situation case study is more appropriate.

Determining if it Is a Good Topic

Not all stories make good case studies, however. At this point, you may have an idea or a story in mind, but may be unsure about the feasibility of turning that story into a case study. In his book *Start with a Story: The Case Study Method of Teaching College Science*, Herreid (2006) presents basic information on the characteristics of good case studies. Consider these characteristics when determining whether your story would make a good case study. These guidelines can apply to all types of case studies, although you will probably realize that some are more appropriate to certain types of case studies.

- Good case studies tell interesting stories. They should revolve around issues that are of interest to the reader. Each should include a beginning and middle, and some may include an end (although sometimes, especially in decision and in-basket case studies, it is the responsibility of the reader to come to a conclusion).
- Good cases should have compelling issues. Whether made up or based on actual fact, the case should be real enough so that the reader is able to get involved.
- Good cases are relevant and should be set in the present. Again, this is important in capturing the interest of the reader. Cases have to be relevant to problems being solved today. For example, it would be difficult for students to relate to a case study involving the use of typewriters in a 1960s office secretarial pool—even if those

details were not the main focus of the case. Cases should be situations that the reader may be familiar with or may actually encounter.

- Good case studies include empathetic main characters. Herreid (2006) notes that creating empathy makes the story more engaging and provides personal details of the characters that may influence their decision-making processes. The role and importance of characters in case studies depends on the story being told. Some case studies feature prominent characters in influential positions. In others, characters are secondary to the problem to be solved.

- Good case studies include quotations. To demonstrate, I'll quote Herreid (2006): "There is no better way to understand a situation and to gain empathy for the characters than to hear them speaking in their own voices. Quotations add life and drama to any case. Quotations from documents and letters should be used as well. Quotations give realism" (p. 46). The use of quotations also depends on the type of case study being developed. In some case styles, like the in-basket exercise, it is more difficult to incorporate the use of spoken quotes. In these situations, quotes may be in the form of notes or post-it messages attached to documents. While the use of quotes can certainly add realism to a case study, do not include quotes simply for the sake of doing so. They should only be included if they add some type of value to the case study. There are many good case studies that do not include quotes.

- Good case studies should be functional. They should be learning tools and should be appropriate in helping students learn about the subject being studied.

- Good cases should involve conflict. They should include areas for debate, issues for discussion, and details that may be problematic. They should be able to be examined through multiple perspectives. They should include variables that cause students to pause and consider different options. A case study on which everyone agrees on the final solution is probably not an effective case study.

- Good cases should require the reader to develop a decision. This is true of both exemplary and problem situation case studies, although problem situation case studies tend to place more of an emphasis on decisions, whereas exemplary case studies focus more on processes (however, exemplary case studies require the reader to consider decisions made by characters in the case). Good cases do not allow students to avoid issues. Rather, they force students to address issues and come up with solutions. Some case studies include an element of time in them—"the project manager had three hours to determine a course of action in order to meet his deadline," for example.

- Good cases should be somewhat generalizable. The point of a good case study is to elicit consideration of responses or course of action, which, in turn, help students to develop their skills in these areas. If a case study is too specific or contains too many details, the reader may not be able to relate it to the real world. The story of an event that happened one time and is likely to never happen again is also not a good candidate for conversion into a case study. Remember that the purpose of case studies is to help readers develop skills that can be used in the future. Readers may be able to address that one-in-a-million scenario case study, but how will doing so help them develop skills they can use?

- Good cases are short. They include enough detail, but not too much. They hold the attention of the reader, and allow the reader to easily review key points. They are not long and boring. If a case study is too long, the author should consider dividing it up into two separate cases. To give you an idea about length, consider that the case studies included in this book average about 750 words (excluding discussion questions or references). There may be situations in which case studies are much longer, but that depends on the circumstance for which they are being written, including the needs of the learner and the topic to be presented.

Characteristics of Good Case Studies (Herreid, 2006)

- Interesting story
- Compelling issue
- Relevant and set in the present
- Empathetic main characters
- Include quotations
- Functional
- Involve conflict
- Require the reader to come up with a decision
- Somewhat generalizable
- Short in length

Figure 4.4.

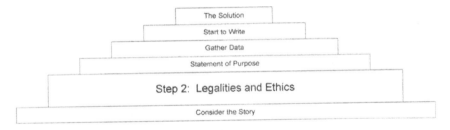

Figure 4.5.

How does your case study idea stack up against the checklist above? While your idea does not have to meet all of the recommendations noted here, good case study ideas will meet a majority of these recommendations. If your idea meets few of these qualifications, you might consider adjusting it or choosing an entirely new idea.

STEP 2: LEGALITIES AND ETHICS

Are there ethical and legal issues associated with the situation you are interested in developing into a case study? As noted in chapter 1, some authors believe that case studies must contain only real, and no made up information. However, in some disciplines, that is not possible for ethical and legal reasons. If you are working in education, you may have to change personal information such as names, dates, and locations in order to protect the identity of the individuals in the case. Some states have laws regarding student records and privacy, so be sure you have a clear understanding of these laws before proceeding. If you have questions on these issues, be sure to check with your school's administration before moving forward.

Legal issues aside, you may have ethical obligations to protect those students or clients who are potential characters in your case study. Consider the ethical ramifications of preparing a case study that may clearly identify characters, locations, or situations. How would that identification affect them, and how might it affect entities like other present and future clients or the reputation of the organization in the community? You might consider changing some details to protect yourself, your organization, and the privacy of others. Or you might consider choosing another topic.

STEP 3: STATEMENT OF PURPOSE

Upon choosing the type of case study to be written, it is helpful to write a one or two-sentence purpose statement about the situation (or at least consider the purpose in your mind). This statement should contain the

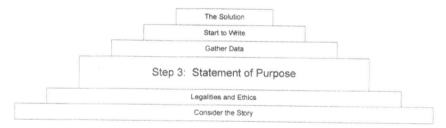

Figure 4.6.

"hook", or the issue to be examined. It should also contain the type of case study you are writing. It should be written in broad and objective fashion, and should not include specifics, suggest solutions, or recommend courses of action. Writing this statement will help guide you through the next steps in the process. Some examples of purpose statements follow:

- This situational case study will examine how training needs are assessed in the customer service department of a retail establishment.
- This complex case study will look at the variety of issues associated with low-literacy adult learners in basic literacy programs.
- This decision case study will help participants hone their prioritization and decision making skills as trainers in a fast-paced hospital environment.

Writing, or at least thinking about, a purpose statement at this point will help keep you on track as you work through the next steps of the process.

STEP 4: GATHER DATA

After you have considered the case study checklist, legal and ethical issues, and have written your statement of purpose, you are ready to gather information that describes the scenario. During this stage of the process, the focus should be on simply gathering data—not in the analysis or consideration of how the case will be pieced together. Data can be gathered from a variety of sources, including personal observations, interviews, records, test scores, and many others (Campoy, 2005). The type and variety of sources used in this step will depend on the type of case study to be written. Complex and decision case studies may contain data from more sources than situation case studies, which may be written sim-

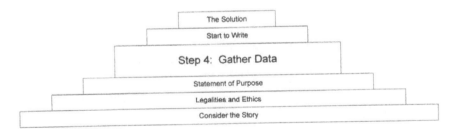

The Solution

Start to Write

Step 4: Gather Data

Statement of Purpose

Legalities and Ethics

Consider the Story

Figure 4.7.

ply as narratives based on personal observation. Either way, the focus at this stage should be on simply gathering the data. Making judgments and evaluations about the data at this point may result in the writing of a biased and ineffective case study. Evaluating data at this stage may also bias authors, which will affect their ability to be objective in the gathering of additional data. If authors have predetermined conclusions about the scenario at this point, they are more likely to ignore data that conflicts with those conclusions and to emphasize data that concurs.

Even experienced case study writers have to continually reflect on their own writing at this stage of the process. It is easy to write in a way that leads the reader down a path of the writer's choice; however, that is not the goal in designing an effective case study. Consider the words and phrases used as you go about the data gathering process. Are your notes written objectively or with a slant toward one conclusion or another? Are you making generalizations, either positive or negative, about characters in the scenario, or are you focusing on facts and specifics? Remember that there is a difference between your own objectivity as a case writer and the opinions of your data sources. Accurately documenting the opinions of people who may become characters in the case study is important. Data collected from those characters in interviews may be biased, and in these cases, it is important to preserve the opinions of others as they are.

Ten Second Tip

Start by gathering data on your case study without analyzing it. Analyzing too early in the process may affect your ability to write an effective case study.

Figure 4.8.

STEP 5: START TO WRITE

After the data is gathered, it is time to return to the issue or problem that will be the focus of your case study. This issue or problem was most likely defined in the statement of purpose in Step 3 of this process. Going forward, the data collected in the previous step should be organized so that it supports the problem or issue itself (Campoy, 1999). However, not all of the data gathered in Step 4 should be used in the development of the case study. Data that supports the problem, offers explanation, and provides valuable information should be included. Depending on the nature of the case study, superfluous data may be included as well. Remember that the type of case study you are writing will influence the amount of data included in the case.

At this time, the actual writing of the case study can begin. Data points collected in the prior step can be woven together to form the story line of the case study. At this stage, it is important to remain focused on the problem or the issue to be described, and to build a supporting network of information that can be used to address that problem or describe the issue in the appropriate level of detail. Again, remember to consider the words used when you write your case. The way in which you present people and situations in your case can easily bias the reader, or can lead the reader to one solution or another. This is not the way to write an effective case study. Information should be presented objectively, so that readers can use their own experience and knowledge to come up with recommendations and solutions by incorporating that experience and knowledge with the facts of the case.

While there is no one correct way to write a case study, Herreid (2006) presents a sample outline for the writing of case studies (see Figure 4.10).

Figure 4.11 illustrates the case study format discussed above. Note that with regard to detail, it goes from general to specific. Start your case study with big-picture information on the situation, then gradually work your way to the specific details of the case.

Figure 4.9.

Sample Outline for a Case Study (Herried, 2006)

Introduction: Consists of a single paragraph that includes information on the decision maker (name, title, role in the organization, for example). The setting is introduced, including the time and place. The problem or issue facing the main character is noted at the end of the first paragraph.

Background: Background on the organization as a whole is presented in this section.

Immediate Organization: Information on the department or organization in which the situation takes place (or in which the main character works) is presented in this section. Details about the actual issue to be faced may be introduced toward the end of this section.

Specific problem: Details of the specific problem are found in this section. This is often one of the longer sections of a case study.

Alternatives: Alternatives being considered by the main character, or by others in the organization (as they may be different) are discussed here.

Conclusions: Final thoughts or pieces of information about the case are noted here. This short section also gives details about timelines (when a decision has to be made, for example).

Figure 4.10.

Keep in mind that the format you use when writing your case study will depend on the type of case study you are writing. The format noted by Herreid (2006) seems most appropriate for exercise or situational-type case studies. Parts of it can be used for decision or critical incident case studies as well.

When writing your case study, always remember your audience. Factors such as the reading level and problem-solving abilities of that audience should dictate the level at which you write the case.

The amount of data you include depends on the type of case study you are writing. As a general rule, include enough data so the case can be dis-

Normal Case Outline
(Mauffette-Leenders, Erskine & Leenders, 2005)

- The opening paragraph
- Specific problem or decision
- Organization background (structure, products, industry, competition, services, history, financial situation)
- Specific area of interest (marketing, finance, operations, other)
- Alternatives (optional)
- Conclusion (task, deadline)
- Specific problem or decision

Figure 4.11.

Ten Second Tip

When you are writing a case study, remember to keep in mind the type of study you are writing and the audience for whom you are writing. That will determine many factors and parameters about what you write.

Figure 4.12.

cussed and debated from multiple perspectives. Include a variety of elements that may be relevant to the way the case is addressed. Remember that the approach readers take when working through a case study differs depending on their education and experience. Some may focus on facts, while others focus on feelings. Some may focus on environmental issues, while others may look at the case from a political viewpoint. Some may look at procedures while others look at people. Including enough data on a variety of topics will help to ensure healthy debate on the case.

STEP 6: THE SOLUTION

As noted in the first chapter of this book, one of the issues that is difficult for students to understand with case study exercises is the fact that there are not necessarily right or wrong answers or solutions for them. Do you

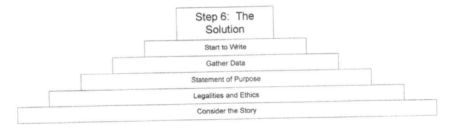

Figure 4.13.

want to include a solution to your case? In some cases, solutions are included and in others, they are not. The determination on whether to include a solution depends on the type of case study you are writing. In some cases, such as in-basket exercises, there are no pat or correct solutions. Rather, the solution is in how each individual deals with the information presented. Often in situational-type cases, there are solutions, but those solutions are in the form of what actually happened: what course of action was taken by the main character in the case, for example.

It is often impossible to determine whether or not the course of action actually taken was, in fact, the best way to proceed. Is a student who chooses a different solution wrong? Maybe that student's solution would have been better, had it been the course of action taken in the real situation. It is also possible that the instructor or facilitator may find fault with the solution, and the solution may become a case study in itself. Solutions for case studies can certainly be included in those studies. They can be included at the end of the case study, or as supplementary pieces that can be shared with readers after discussion of the case. The determination on whether or not to include a solution depends on the case itself, and rests with the author. What is not in doubt is the value of the debriefing process and the discussion of these issues as part of the process of working through a case study.

CONCLUSION

While the steps above can help potential case study authors work through the process, a common theme noted in these steps is that the action taken in each step depends on the type of case study to be written. These are not hard and fast rules for developing case studies. Rather, they are guidelines that can be followed in the fashion that the author believes appropriate, depending on the situation and the type of case study to be written.

The writing of case studies can be an effective educational tool. This chapter highlights the steps involved in writing a case study. With the proper story in mind, following these steps can result in the development of a case study that can ultimately be addressed as an instructional tool itself.

REFERENCES

Armistead, C. (1984, February). How useful are case studies? *Training and Development Journal, 38*(2), 75-77.

Campoy, R. (2005). *Case study analysis in the classroom: Becoming a reflective teacher.* Thousand Oaks, CA: Sage.

Carter, C. (1999). What is a case? What is not a case? In M. A. Lundeberg, B. B. Levin, & H. L. Harrington (Eds.), *Who learns what from cases and how?* (pp. 165-175). Mahwah, NJ: Erlbaum.

Herreid, C. F. (2006). *Start with a story: The case method of teaching college science.* Arlington, VA: National Science Teachers Foundation Press.

ABOUT THE AUTHOR

Steven W. Schmidt is an assistant professor of adult education and the adult education program coordinator at East Carolina University, in Greenville, North Carolina. He holds PhD and MS degrees in adult education from the University of Wisconsin–Milwaukee and a bachelor of business administration degree from the University of Wisconsin–Whitewater. Schmidt's major areas of research and writing activity include workplace learning, cultural competence, and online teaching and learning.

Schmidt is currently a member of the executive board of the American Association for Adult and Continuing Education. His research studies have been published in a variety of journals, and he has made presentations at national and international conferences. Additionally, he serves on editorial review boards of several major journals that focus on adult education and human resource development.

Prior to joining the faculty of East Carolina University, Schmidt spent 18 years in the Fortune 500, working in the areas of marketing, public relations, and employee training and development. He is the recipient of the 2009 Early Career Award from the National Commission of Professors of Adult Education. This annual award recognizes outstanding achievement in teaching and research by a new professor.

ABOUT THE CONTRIBUTORS

Brian A. Altman is a doctoral student in the Department of Administrative Leadership at the University of Wisconsin-Milwaukee in Milwaukee, WI.

Bo Chang is a PhD in lifelong education administration and policy at the University of Georgia, in Athens, GA.

Simone C. O. Conceicao, PhD, is an associate professor of adult Education at the University of Wisconsin-Milwaukee in Milwaukee, WI.

Thomas D. Cox, EdD, is an assistant professor of adult and higher Education at the University of Houston–Victoria in Victoria, TX.

Denise Cumberland is the director of consumer insights and innovations at YUM Brands in Louisville, KY and also teaches at the University of Louisville.

Barbara J. Daley, PhD, is professor of adult education and chair of the Administrative Leadership Department at the University of Wisconsin-Milwaukee in Milwaukee, WI.

Jeremy Dickerson, EdD, is an assistant professor of business and information technologies education at East Carolina University in Greenville, NC

Kaye B. Dotson, EdD, is an assistant professor of library science at East Carolina University in Greenville, NC

Kylie P. Dotson-Blake, PhD, is an assistant professor of counselor education at East Carolina University in Greenville, NC

Patrick Finnessy, PhD, is the executive director of Teaching Out and an adjunct instructor at the University of Toronto in Toronto, ON.

Julie Gedro, MBA, PHR, EdD, is an associate professor of business, management, and economics at SUNY Empire State College in Syracuse, New York.

Rajashi Ghosh, PhD, is an assistant professor of human resource development in the School of Education, Goodwin College of Professional Studies at Drexel University in Philadelphia, PA.

Rod P. Githens, PhD, is an assistant professor in the Department of Leadership, Foundations, and Human Resource Education at the University of Louisville in Louisville, KY.

J. Scott Glass, PhD, is an associate professor and coordinator of the Counselor Education Program at East Carolina University in Greenville, NC.

Ruth Greenburg, PhD, is an associate dean for medical education at the University Of Louisville School Of Medicine in Louisville, KY.

Annette Greer, EdD, is codirector of interdisciplinary studies in the Division of Health Sciences at East Carolina University in Greenville, NC.

Pi-Chi Han, EdD, is an assistant professor in the Division of Educational Leadership and Policy Studies at the University of Missouri–St. Louis in St. Louis, MO.

Catherine Hansman, EdD, is a professor of adult learning and development at Cleveland State University in Cleveland, OH.

Ray K. Haynes, PhD, is an assistant professor of education at Indiana University in Bloomington, IN.

Judy Hill is the coordinator of adult basic education and English as a second language programs at Lenoir Community College in Kinston, NC.

Elizabeth S. Knott, EdD, is an associate professor of adult education at East Carolina University in Greenville, NC.

Martin B. Kormanik, PhD, is the president and CEO of O.D. Systems in Alexandria, VA

Karen H. Miller, PhD, is an associate professor in the Office of Graduate Medical Education at the University Of Louisville School Of Medicine in Louisville, KY.

Vivian W. Mott, PhD, is a professor and chair of the Counselor and Adult/Higher Education Department at East Carolina University in Greenville, NC.

Sunny L. Munn is a doctoral candidate in workforce development and education at The Ohio State University in Columbus, OH.

Amanda Neill is a doctoral candidate in adult education at Pennsylvania State University–Harrisburg and also an enrollment and industrial relations coordinator at Pennsylvania State Great Valley School of Graduate Professional Studies in Malvern, PA.

Kenneth D. Ott, EdD, is an associate professor of adult and career education at Valdosta State University in Valdosta, GA.

Mari Jo Pesch, PhD, is a trainer and organizational development specialist at the University of Colorado Hospital in Denver, CO

Maria (Masha) S. Plakhotnik is a doctoral candidate in adult education and human resource development at Florida International University in Miami, FL.

Tonette S. Rocco, PhD, is an associate professor and program leader of adult education and human resource development at Florida International University in Miami, FL.

Steven W. Schmidt, PhD, is an assistant professor and coordinator of the Adult Education Program at East Carolina University in Greenville, NC.

Shelia Tucker, PhD, is an associate professor of business and information technologies education at East Carolina University in Greenville, NC.

LaVergne, TN USA
22 September 2010
198055LV00001B/56/P